To My Dear
May the
HOPE fi
Love,

# Reflections OF A Hopemonger

# Reflections OF A *Hopemonger*

"…this hope, as an anchor for our souls…"

Aba Cato Andah

DAKPABLI & ASSOCIATES
ACCRA

REFLECTIONS OF A HOPEMONGER



**ISBN: 97899889023 0 8**

**Editor**
Nana Awere Damoah

Book Layout by multiPIXEL Limited
P O Box DC 1965, Dansoman, Accra, Ghana
Email: jkojoyanney@gmail.com
Tel: +233 302 333 502 | +233 246 725 060 | +233 246 210 862

Published by
DAkpabli & Associates
P O Box 7465, Accra North, Accra, Ghana
Tel: +233 264 339 066 | +233 244 704 250 | +233 247 896 375
Email: info@dakpabli.com

## THE IMAGE ON THE COVER DEPICTS A KINTSUGI BOWL

Life is a journey of learning experiences. Reflections of a Hopemonger is part memoir, part guidebook. It is a collection of essays largely based on my personal experiences -- the joys, the triumphs, as well as the mistakes and missteps. Each essay is crafted to contain gold nuggets of wisdom meant to inject hope into the reader.

Perfection is unattainable in this life, and brokenness does not disqualify a piece of art -- or a child of God -- from becoming a masterpiece.

Hence the idea of incorporating Kintsugi into the artwork for the cover. Kintsugi is the Japanese art of repairing broken pottery by mending the areas of breakage with lacquer mixed with powdered gold. So breakage and repair, rather than being disguised, are celebrated as part of the history of an object. God uses brokenness for His glory. Out of brokenness, wondrous beauty can emerge.

# Author Profile

Aba Cato Andah, MBA, MA, LMHC is a psychotherapist in private practice. Originally from Ghana in West Africa, Aba's life and work experiences have been varied and rich. She has lived and worked in Africa, Europe, Canada and the United States. Her career background includes science research, teaching and over a decade as a sales and marketing executive with a multinational pharmaceutical company.

The constant theme in Aba's life and career has been her concern for the well-being of others and her love for imparting information and new insights to encourage people to live more authentic and rewarding lives.

Aba is also a Director of a not-for-profit organization aimed at mental health education and promotion.

Aba is married and has an adult son, a daughter and a daughter-in-law.

*To my parents, with eternal love and gratitude. Your ideals and compassion are my compass.*

*To the memory of KBO, my dear brother-friend.*

## ACKNOWLEDGEMENTS

I am profoundly grateful to my family: Eddie, Archie, Elissa and Sarah. Sharing my personal stories would not have been possible without sharing some of yours. Thank you for allowing me the freedom to do that. Your constant love and encouragement spur me on.

I also owe a debt of gratitude to Dr. Edmund Andah, FRCOG, FACOG and Esi Eduafowa Sey, PhD – my first-pass feedback team. Eddie, you compelled me to let go of my fears and dig deep. And, Esi, you read through the manuscript and gave me detailed feedback in just one weekend! Thank you!

To my amazing reviewers: Auntie Joyce, Charlotte, Ace, Kurankyi, Esi Ansah, Esi Sey, Ekua, Daphne, Kobina and Adeline. I am touched and honored that you took time out of your busy schedules to review this book. Thank you all for 'getting' me and getting the purpose that birthed this book!

To my editor, Nana Awere Damoah of DAkpabli Publishing; I am truly grateful for your support and guidance throughout this process.

Finally, all my thanks goes to the Almighty God for giving me a hopemonger's heart that would not rest until this project was complete. My prayer is that *Reflections of a Hopemonger* blesses everyone who reads it!

# CONTENTS

# FOREWORD

*"A Christian will part with anything rather than his hope; he knows that hope will keep the heart both from aching and breaking, from fainting and sinking; he knows that hope is a beam of God, a spark of glory, and that nothing shall extinguish it till the soul be filled with glory."* – **Thomas Brooks**

This quote by Thomas Brooke sheds additional light on what the author, Aba Cato Andah, seeks to achieve by her incredible book, *Reflections of A Hopemonger.*

*Reflections of A Hopemonger* addresses everyday happenings that could easily be overlooked as trivial, yet which could insidiously contribute to depression, heartache and, possibly, even death. So many of us are going through the stresses that come with everyday life. What better way to reach the hearts of readers than to share personal experiences and real life occurrences; stories that readers can actually relate to and draw inspirations from?

This is exactly what the author has done. She directly addresses these issues by introducing Bible verses to let readers know that the hope she so tenaciously holds on to cannot be gained by one's own strength but by the grace of God.

One of her timeless quotations that really caught my attention is this: ***"I have realized that I need to leave room in my life for God, who is my Shepherd, my Healer, my Provider, my Victory, my Friend, my Restorer and my Peace. It is non- negotiable for me."*** Such a statement could only be made by one who has an intimate relationship with God and is able to relate this divine relationship with everyday life. We could all do with such a relationship as we go through the maze of life and face the inevitable trials and tribulations of life.

*Reflections of a Hopemonger* is indeed a book of encouragement for the many who are determined to hang on their hope in God as the only real anchor in the storms of life.

*Reflections of a Hopemonger* is a must read for both young and old because it addresses in succinct and practical ways, how to embrace life with joy because he or she knows, as Thomas Brook says, that ***"hope is a beam of God, a spark of glory and that nothing shall extinguish it till the soul is filled with glory."***

*Rev. Dr. Joyce Aryee*
*Executive Director*
*Salt and Light Ministeries*
*Ghana*

# Prologue

# Storyteller

*"Oh the mountain where I climbed*
*The valley where I fell*
*You were there all along*
*That's the story I'll tell*
*You brought the pieces together*
*Made me this storyteller*
*Now I know it is well, it is well*
*That's the story I'll tell..."*

– *Morgan Harper Nichols (from the song* "Storyteller"*)*

~~~~~~~~~~~~~~~~~~~~~~~~~

I am a storyteller. Our lives are made up of stories. To tell a story is to tell about life.

The power of a good story lies in its ability to engage people emotionally and intellectually at a deeper level.
~~~~~~~~~~~~~~~~~~~~~~~~~

Stories are bridges that create connections between different people and their experiences. Thus, a good story helps us to know that we are not alone in our experiences.

Most importantly, a good story is one that carries a lesson, which leads us to new insights and a better way of living.

Often, we give the world only snippets of our story, especially on social media. Those snippets tend to be the polished, sanitized versions, not the authentic story. Because our authentic personal stories are seldom pretty or glamorous or flattering as they unfold. More often than not, our authentic stories reveal our character defects. More often than not, our authentic stories unfold with blood, sweat, tears, missteps, failures, persistence, resilience and, ultimately, victory. Sometimes the only victory gained is wisdom and insight to not repeat those mistakes.

But the truth is that it is our imperfect, gritty authentic personal stories that people identify with and actually learn from.

I share my personal stories to educate, to inject hope and to inspire people to dig deeper and make a positive change in their lives. I share my personal stories to let people know that it's okay to be vulnerable and imperfect. Most of all, I share my personal stories to encourage people to build their faith in God.

I have done a lot of soul-searching over the past decade or so, and being a licensed, professional mental health therapist I prided myself on my ability to dig deep emotionally and to embrace my vulnerability. Based on that premise, I set out confidently to write this book.

When I sent my husband my first draft, I waited with bated breath for his feedback. He was underwhelmed. "You're holding back," he said. My first instinct was to become defensive, but then I decided to take his feedback in good faith, and re-read my essays to see if his observations had any merit.

He was right.

My argument had been that I did not want salacious details to overshadow the life lessons that I wanted to highlight in my stories. My other argument was that my life experiences were not just about me; my life and my stories were interwoven with my loved ones, and I wanted to spare them the ordeal of being judged.

But, even as I put forward that last argument, I realized that the full truth was that I was the one who was afraid to reveal too many unflattering details in my stories. I was still a product of my social and cultural conditioning.

I am originally from Ghana, West Africa and my observation is that an individual who shares 'unpalatable' details of their life runs the risk of being viewed as a disgrace or an embarrassment to their family or community. A friend of mine – a vibrant, brilliant, soulful woman and mental health advocate – once shared the story of her personal struggle on social media. And was admonished by her friend, with the words, "Congratulations! You've just succeeded in making everyone think you're psycho."

Among Ghanaians, we often find out only after someone has died that they had been suffering from cancer or some other serious health condition. This is evidence of a culture of secrecy, is it not?

One example I can think of had to do with a president of Ghana, who passed away, seemingly suddenly. Reports that surfaced after his death, however, indicated that he had been very unwell for a while, as a result of a progressive cancer. But this was not officially made known to the public while he was alive, although rumors had been swirling. In fact, an infamous video footage showcased the president jogging, as evidence of his physical fitness following what was described as a 'routine medical checkup'. A month later he was dead.

Perhaps there were legitimate reasons behind the cover up. But it left me wondering to what extent admitting to physical illness or emotional vulnerability is seen as a sign of weakness among Ghanaians? And if so, could this not be a major reason why so many people are isolated and in denial about their challenges?

As a mental health advocate, I mentor Akua (not her real name), a beautiful young lady whose life was derailed about 5 years ago when she was diagnosed with bipolar disorder in her last semester of university. Akua is still struggling to get herself back on track. She is inconsistent with taking her medications as prescribed and is still struggling to accept that she suffers from bipolar disorder. A sentiment she has often expressed is this: "I know I'm not bipolar...people are always trying to make it seem like I'm weak and that they are better than me..." Akua's ingrained perception was that that mental illness and vulnerability make a person weak and less than.

My theory may or may not hold true for other countries and cultural groups. But what I can say, with certainty, is this: secrets kill.

It's time to break the culture of secrecy and taboo. It takes courage to share our authentic personal stories. And whenever we do, we create amazing opportunities to replace ignorance with insight; to replace stigma with education and to replace the feeling of isolation with the fellowship of our authentic warrior stories.

Kudos to the brave souls who have shared about how diabetes or autism or mental illness or cancer or single parenthood has affected their lives. Even more kudos to them for creating safe open dialogues and support networks. You are the real MVPs. By sharing your authentic personal stories, you have been lifesavers.

Author Brené Brown made this profound statement: "When we deny our stories, they define us. When we own our stories, we get to write a brave new ending."

So, let's not hold back on sharing our stories.

Here are some of mine…

# Pearls of Wisdom

## *Diamond Incentive*

**"I can do all things through Christ who strengthens me." - Philippians 4:13 NKJV**

**"...the desires of the diligent are fully satisfied." - Proverbs 13:4 NIV**

~~~~~~~~~~~~~~~~~~~~~~~~~

From the moment I decided to write this book, I found myself beset periodically with self-doubt that left me feeling unmotivated and discouraged. Would I be able to finish the book? Would people consider it to be a worthwhile venture? Would people buy it?

But, recently, I found a letter in my archives that instantly refocused and re-energized me.
~~~~~~~~~~~~~~~~~~~~~~~~~

The letter was from a high-end jewelry store, to my boss. It was about the flawless diamond I had just won at work.

The back story: It was 2001 and I had just been transferred from my marketing job at Head Office with GlaxoSmithKline Pharmaceuticals in London to a new sales position in Newcastle, England.

I had never worked in sales and I felt insecure about my abilities. Most of the Representatives in that area were experienced, with solid customer relationships and long histories of sales success. I was new to the area, a rookie in sales and a black woman with a foreign accent.

But everything changed for me at our regional sales meeting that year. I held my breath in awe as an exquisitely beautiful diamond was projected onto a huge screen. The Regional Vice President announced that it was flawless diamond and it would be awarded to the winner of the 'Diamond Incentive'.

In that moment I knew that I had to have that diamond.

The company had just launched a new medication and each Rep was asked to devise and implement a strategy to "flawlessly" grow the business. Hence the prize of a "flawless" diamond.

My simple desire to own that diamond was the fuel I needed to creatively devise my strategy. But beyond that, I now remembered that the key to my success was a solid and consistent work ethic – whether I felt inspired that day or not!

Over the next 3 months, I was so immersed and engaged with working consistently and "flawlessly" that I didn't focus on the areas where I had a disadvantage. What did I have to lose? I went for it and gave it my all.

And, against my perceived odds, I was the winner of the 'Diamond Incentive'! The value of that flawless diamond was equivalent to an almost 10% increase in my annual salary in 2001.

But the value of the life lesson that my flawless diamond gave to me? Priceless.

LONDON

167 New Bond Street, London W1S 4AR
Telephone 020 7493 6767 Facsimile 020 7491 0384

*28th March, 2001*

Mr. Paul
Whitley Bay,
Tyne and Wear,
NE26 3PQ

Dear Paul,

I am delighted to enclose the prize of a brilliant cut diamond for Aba Andah

I have been in direct contact with her regarding the cut. As a jewellers, our recommendation to her, given the size of the stone, was that the diamond should be brilliant cut, and she was very happy for us to proceed with that. Aba said that she would like to mount the diamond into a ring, and thinks it best to arrange for that to be done locally. I agree that this would be the ideal scenario, as there will be a lot of meeting and discussion regarding the design etc.

In the box enclosed, you will find a velvet pouch, which contains a small box which carries the diamond itself. I have also enclosed a leather ring box, which Aba can use for the ring when it is complete.

I do hope that Aba receives great pleasure from this lovely prize.

Please do not hesitate to contact me if we can be of any further assistance.

With kind regards,

Carol Butterworth

*Carol Butterworth*
*Senior Account Manager*
*Corporate Division*

Asprey & Garrard Limited. Registered in England No.103844 at 167 New Bond Street, London W1S 4AR

# Collateral Damage

**"People at war with themselves will always cause collateral damage in the lives of those around them." – John Mark Green**

**"If you pick up one end of the stick, you also pick up the other." – Ethiopian proverb**

~~~~~~~~~~~~~~~~~~~~~~~~~~

I dreamed a dream yesterday. I was cruising down the road in my shiny new red Corvette convertible. The sunset was magnificent, the breeze was perfect, the car was driving smoothly and I was on top of the world.

All of sudden an old, banged up car pulled up from nowhere. Approaching at full speed and with seeming intent, the car crashed into the back panel of my Corvette, causing serious damage. Then, the driver backed up and just drove off!
~~~~~~~~~~~~~~~~~~~~~~~~~~

Initially I was caught off guard, but as I processed what had just happened, I felt my blood begin to boil. I became furious. My instinct was to chase the car down and read the driver the riot act. Did he really think he could get away with this?

But as I revved up my engine to go after him, I suddenly realized that my daughter was standing in the middle of the road, walking towards me.

I faced a dilemma, whether or not to chase after the car. I didn't want the guy to get away. Yet if I had allowed myself to speed up in that moment, I would have hit and injured my precious daughter.

I decided against chasing the car, because I didn't want to inadvertently hurt my beloved daughter. My daughter's life and well-being were infinitely more important to me than a dent to my car.

Damage to a car is fixable. Or even if not, a car can always be replaced. My precious daughter, however, is irreplaceable.

**Collateral damage** is any death, injury, or other damage inflicted on an unintended target.

P.S.: This story is not actually about red Corvettes involved in road accidents.

Next time, before you physically or emotionally abuse your spouse, think about the collateral damage – the emotional trauma to your child because of what they witness or hear.

Next time, before you decide to let out a barrage of insults about your child's other parent, within earshot of your child, think about the collateral damage. Your words will also wound your child and strip them of their self-esteem!

Next time, before you decide not to pay child support because of misplaced priorities or because you are angry with your ex, think about the collateral damage. Is there ever a reason that justifies abandoning your child to financial hardship?

Next time, before you decide, for no real reason except anger and spite, to prevent your ex from seeing their child, think about the collateral damage. Have you considered the acute heartache it causes a child who is separated from a loving parent?

Next time, before you give in to the temptation to make a choice that is unethical or illegal, think about the collateral damage. Is it worth potentially losing the reputation that you worked hard to build in your profession or community? How would a possible scandal affect your loved ones? And what about the risk of losing your soul, if you go down that path?

Next time, the question we all should ask ourselves is this: *Who or what are we sacrificing in this quest to fulfill an impulsive desire?*

***"There are, it may be, so many kinds of voices...and none of them is without signification." – 1 Corinthians 14:10 KJV***

***"We demolish arguments and every pretension that sets itself up against the knowledge of God, and we take captive every thought to make it obedient to Christ." –*** **2 Corinthians 10:5NIV**

~~~~~~~~~~~~~~~~~~~~~~~~~~

Disclosure: I hear "so many kinds" of voices. But before I elaborate, please allow me to clarify. I don't physically hear the voices. I don't have auditory hallucinations that may be associated with some disorders of mental health. And yet, the voices I 'hear' are as real to me as these words that I write.

As a Christian, I do not for one second doubt the devil's intention to place temptations, trials and confusion in our
~~~~~~~~~~~~~~~~~~~~~~~~~~

lives for the sole purpose of derailing us from being our best selves. However, I also think that many of us put too much emphasis on the devil at the expense of taking full responsibility for our thoughts, motivations and behaviors.

So, while the devil is indeed one of the powerful negative voices and influences in our lives, my focus here is in the voices that come from within *myself*. With time and maturity, I've learned to recognize these voices.

I've also learned that when I refuse to give audience to the voices, or when I challenge these voices with counter arguments based on truth, they have no choice but to die down.

The different voices have different agendas in my life. Each voice, when it speaks, elicits an emotional response from me. And each voice, if left unchallenged, is persuasive enough to sway me in the direction of its bidding. I think of the different voices as different frequency bands on a radio. The more I tune into a particular voice's wavelength, the more dominant that voice becomes. But when I challenge or tune out a voice, that voice then fades out.

Let me introduce you to some of my voices...

*Myopic Voice* is rooted in selfishness and routinely refuses to consider a situation from different perspectives, or its possible impact on the people in my life.

*Impulsive Voice* persuades me to go after short-term gratification at the expense of what is in my long-term best interest.

*Voice of Self-Deception* camouflages the voices of deeper, hidden emotions that I am reluctant to acknowledge. Voice of Self-Deception suppresses my authentic self. Voice of Self-Deception tricks me into believing the most socially acceptable reason as my excuse for taking a particular action, instead of being honest about my true intentions. For example, I might decline an invitation to an event, telling the host and fooling myself into believing that it is only because I have a schedule conflict. But the underlying truth may have been that I just don't want to attend because of any of the following reasons:

- I just don't want to go
- I don't think I would enjoy myself
- I know I will meet an individual at the event who aggravates me.

Note to self: it's perfectly okay to just say, "Sorry, I won't be able to make it."

The only way I can challenge and tune out Voice of Self-Deception is for me to examine myself and be willing to embrace fearless self-honesty.

Whenever I successfully strip away the Voice of Self-Deception, then *Voices of My Flesh* become audible. These include: *Voice of Anger, Voice of Resentment, Voice of Fear, Voice of Pain, Voice of Damaged Pride, Voice of Ulterior Motive, Voice of Shame, Voice of Rejection, Voice of Self-Condemnation* and *Voice of 'Not Good Enough'*. Individually and collectively, these Voices of the Flesh condemn me, erode my self-esteem, sabotage my relationships and keep me mired in hopelessness, fear, hurt, discouragement and a victim mindset.

At this point another voice tries to enter the mix. This is an external 'voice' that whispers further accusations designed to make me feel too condemned, hopeless and discouraged to reach out to God. The Bible refers to Satan as the *accuser of the brethren* and I call this *Voice of the Accuser.*

Thank God that these negating voices are not the only voices that call out to me!

I also have *Voice of Truth*, which is the voice of God. Through experience, I've learned to pick out the ways the voice of God talks to me. Primarily I hear the Voice of Truth from reading and meditating on the Word of God. When I am consistent with this practice, Voice of Truth becomes the strongest voice in my head, and it more easily challenges and drowns out the negative voices. The litmus test in identifying Voice of Truth is that it is completely congruent with the biblical principles by which I choose to live my life. If a voice contradicts the word of God, or encourages me to go along a line of thinking that results in resentful, hateful, unwholesome thoughts, then I know that it is not Voice of Truth. Voice of Truth convicts me where I have done wrong; however Voice of Truth never condemns me. Voice of Truth always empowers me to see that I have the power and the ability to choose my response to any unfavorable situation like the winner that I am.

When I regularly tune in to Voice of Truth, it enables me to also hear *Voice of Highest Self*. Voice of Highest Self stays true to my principles, regardless of prevailing circumstances. Voice of Highest Self, in collaboration with Voice of Truth, sets me on the path of God's Perfect Will for my life. When I work with Voice of Highest Self, I am resilient, positive, and unstoppable.

**Tested**

It was early spring, 1998 in Cambridge, England. I had been a stay-at-home mom for the first nine months of my son's life. I had thoroughly enjoyed that season of my life and was now looking forward to launching a new career. I had been offered my dream job with a great income, opportunities for growth, and a company I was excited to work for.

We considered various options for childcare, eventually deciding to hire an Au Pair. After weeks of preparation and paperwork, we finally got to meet our new Au Pair! She had a kind, engaging smile and my son immediately took to her. My initial excitement was unabated after several days. The Au Pair handled my son wonderfully and kept to the schedule I had given her, to my delight and satisfaction.

About a week after the Au Pair arrived, she began to experience flu-like symptoms and a couple of days after that, dropped a bombshell on us.

"I'm pregnant," she announced. "It's unplanned, I'm not with the father, and I do not want to go through with the pregnancy," she adamantly stated. "Please don't send me away. I want to stay and be your Au Pair."

As I processed her news, the Voices began to kick into full gear.

Voice of Highest Self immediately and strongly reminded me of the pro-life biblical principles from which I draw my moral code. It compelled me to talk to the agency and send the Au Pair away.

But at this point, Myopic Voice began to speak, louder than Voice of Highest Self. Myopic Voice focused on the time, money and effort it had taken to arrange for the Au Pair, and about how absolutely inconvenient it would be to send her away. Myopic Voice hounded me with the startling reality that I was about to start a new job, and had no Plan B for childcare.

Then, Voice of Self-Deception chimed in: "This is all her decision, how is this *your* sin?"

Finally, Voice of Ulterior Motive summed up the arguments from the negative voices. "Listen," Voice of Ulterior Motive said, persuasively. "You worked so hard to arrange for this Au Pair. You are not the one terminating the pregnancy. Just look the other way, let her do what she wants to do, and then carry on as planned."

And so, I tuned out the Voice of Highest Self, and looked the other way. I made her soup when she got back from the clinic and gave her several days off to recover. And the whole thing was behind us. Life quickly went back to normal.

A few weeks later, I got home from work a little earlier than usual. The warm inviting aroma of freshly cooked dinner hit me as soon as I entered the house, and I felt incredibly lucky to have that kind of help. The baby was napping downstairs, so I quietly took off my coat and began sorting through the day's mail.

After about five minutes, it struck me that the house was oddly quiet; the Au Pair would always come out to greet me when I arrived home. So, I went up to her room and knocked on her door. When there was no response after several attempts, I opened her door.

Her room was bare. She had packed up and was gone.

"Oh, no!!" Voice of Pain screamed.

"I definitely didn't see this coming", Myopic Voice exclaimed.

"What are you going to do now?" Voice of Despair asked.

"It serves you right! You have blood on your hands!" Voice of the Accuser chided.

"Don't condemn yourself", Voice of Truth said. "You learned a valuable lesson. Henceforth, don't compromise your values." Voice of Truth then continued, "My child, you are forgiven. Know that nothing will separate you from My love. So, don't fret; you will be okay. I am the Provider, and I will lead you to the childcare that I had planned for you. Remember that Home Day Care you liked that was full the last time you checked? Why don't you give the lady a call again?"

## The Wounds of a Friend

**"Faithful are the wounds of a friend, but the kisses of an enemy are lavish and deceitful."– Proverbs 27:6 AMPC**

**"Don't make friends who are comfortable to be with. Make friends who will force you to lever yourself up." – Thomas J. Watson**

~~~~~~~~~~~~~~~~~~~~~~~~

On the surface, my sister-friend Ama and I were like chalk and cheese. Whereas I preferred the company of a small group of intimate friends, Ama was bold, vivacious and popular; the life and soul of the party, and with a wicked sense of humor to boot. But Ama and I 'got' each other. We have always had a lot to talk about and plenty to laugh about. Within a short time of meeting, in Lower Sixth Form at
~~~~~~~~~~~~~~~~~~~~~~~~

Achimota School, we formed a strong bond that, thirty-five years later, has endured the test of time.

As the years went by, we found ourselves both newlyweds living in the United Kingdom. In the course of time, we were both expectant mothers, with our due dates six weeks apart. As one might imagine, we became a major support system for each other. Together, we navigated the experiences of marriage, pregnancy and first-time motherhood.

We spoke daily; frequently exchanging tips on caring for our babies. Our conversations were always punctured with hoots of laughter; I think Ama may have missed her calling as a standup comedian, because her wit and comedic timing were simply impeccable. I remember one conversation where I proudly announced to Ama (using a motherhood guru-like tone) that I used a Q-tip dipped in baby oil to gently clean my son's ears. And I enquired what method she used. Without missing a beat, she quipped "I use *ntesuo* (spit) and nothing!"

One afternoon Ama had come to visit, and we were both nursing our sons. We were both preparing to go back to work after maternity leave. I had been trying to transition my son to bottle-feeding but he did not like it at all and frequently rejected the bottle. Eventually I invested in a top-of-the-line feeding bottle brand whose main selling point was that their teats were designed to feel exactly like a mother's nipple. But my son rejected that bottle, too.

So, that day as we were both nursing, I shared my woes with Ama, frustrated that my baby was again refusing this expensive brand, with the teat shaped exactly like a nipple. Ama paused for a moment, looked down at my bosom and then back up at me, askance. And then she dryly responded, "But you, do you think that *your* nipple looks anything like that teat?"

I was initially taken aback at the bluntness of her response, but then I burst out laughing at the realization that she was absolutely correct! Truly, that teat was shaped nothing like my nipple!

I 'heard' Ama that day. Her message: don't spend money blindly on a product just because it's a major brand name. Do your due diligence and be discerning in your purchases.

Beyond feeding bottles, Ama's lesson has served me well, through the years.

We all need friends in our lives who are positive, supportive, and good fun. We are doubly blessed when they love us enough to always tell us the truth, even when it's not easy to listen to.

True friends help us grow. True friends are a gift.

# It's Not What You Call Me, But What I Answer To

"We all lose when bullying and personal attacks become a substitute for genuine conversation and principled disagreement." – Alicia Garza

"It's not what you call me, but what I answer to." – African Proverb

"We must forever conduct our struggle on the high plane of dignity and discipline." – Martin Luther King Jr.

~~~~~~~~~~~~~~~~~~~~~~~~~
~~~~~~~~~~~~~~~~~~~~~~~~~

Dear Younger Me,

Arguably, few experiences are more disconcerting for you than when someone unfairly characterizes or falsely accuses you.
In the immediate aftermath of such an attack, you experience a frozen, deer-in-headlights feeling of shock. And then, rising indignation as your blood figuratively begins to boil.

Your attacker struck a nerve.

If you paid attention to your body, you would have noticed your heart beating faster or heat rising in your face. That is because your body is experiencing stress. Physiologically, your body is shifting into 'fight or flight' mode; as though you have encountered an actual physical threat.

Younger Self, you need to know that stress affects how your brain processes information and, ultimately, how you will respond. If you allow yourself to react in the heat of the moment, you will lash out like a wounded lion, but nothing will be resolved.

Let's reflect on the times you did lash out. Did you think you really 'won' in those situations? Or, by reacting impulsively, did you actually take your opponent's bait and ultimately march to the beat of their drum? They were looking to get a rise out of you, and they got you. You lowered yourself down to their level. Where is the victory in that, Younger Self?

Don't react in the heat of the moment. There is another choice. Respond rather than react. To respond appropriately, you need to step back, assess the situation, and then thoughtfully measure out your response.

***Step Back:*** Breathe deeply for several minutes. Take your mind off the heat of the moment by engaging in another activity. Go for a walk. Give yourself a few hours to completely calm down. In fact, as aggravating as the situation may be, if it's not urgent, you may even choose to sleep on it before you decide how to respond. A dear friend of mine once told me that, where possible, she chooses not to react for 24 hours. She says it gives her time to really think things through before she decides on her response. The truth is that many verbal attacks and accusations actually do not need an immediate reaction. And you will find it remarkable the difference that rest, a decent meal and stepping away from a situation for a few hours can have on your perspective.

***Assess the Situation***: Figure out how the situation made you feel. Angry? Indignant? Embarrassed? Hurt? Betrayed? Humiliated? Identifying how you feel is an important step because we cannot overcome that which we cannot acknowledge. Only when you have acknowledged what you are feeling, can you deal with those feelings.

Know that you must always look within yourself and upwards to God, to heal your hurts and negative emotions. Insults and vengeful behavior have never restored anyone's pride or lifted up their self-esteem.

When the accusation is a direct attack on your integrity and accountability, you do need to set the record straight. Plan your response with logical, well-developed arguments.

Sometimes, people just want to get a rise out of you; to ridicule you, diminish you and embarrass you. Be aware of such unsavory characters and refuse to take their bait! Often, the accusation is nothing but a small-minded, trifling attack from a small-minded, trifling person. In those situations, ask yourself whether it is even worth your while to dignify them with a response. Here is an important fact of life to be aware of: when there's nothing to defend, there's nothing to defend! You owe that person nothing. If they want to spend their time bad mouthing you, that is their problem.

***Measure Out Your Response***: Never forget that a very valid choice may be to choose to not respond to your haters. Eleanor Roosevelt said: *"What other people think of me is none of my business."* However, if you decide that it is necessary to respond, let your answer to these three questions be a "yes" in considering your crafted response:

1. Am I obligated to set the record straight?
2. Is my proposed response consistent with my value system (e.g. Truth, Integrity, Respect etc.)?
3. Would I be proud of my response 10 years from now?

I am counting on you to do the right thing for us!

Love,
Older Wiser You

~~~~~~~~~~~~~~~~~~~~~~~~~

***If you can keep your head when all about you***
***Are losing theirs and blaming it on you...***
***Yours is the Earth and everything that's in it,***
***And – which is more – you'll be a Man, my son!***

***(From the poem "IF" by Rudyard Kipling)***

(Disclaimer: Rudyard Kipling's "IF" poem was apt for this essay, however his controversial views do not reflect mine.)
~~~~~~~~~~~~~~~~~~~~~~~~~

## *The Worst is Over*

**"For we were saved in this hope, but hope that is seen is not hope; for why does one still hope for what he sees? But if we hope for what we do not see, we eagerly wait for it with perseverance." – Romans 8: 24-25 NKJV**

**"They say a person needs just three things to be truly happy in this world: someone to love, something to do, and something to hope for." – Tom Bodett**

~~~~~~~~~~~~~~~~~~~~~~~~~~

A few years ago, I went through a difficult period. And one day, feeling particularly overwhelmed, I did what any mature, confident, wise woman would do – I called my Daddy on the phone and cried my heart out!

I don't recall much of the conversation beyond the fact that my words came tumbling out between deep, breathless sobs,
~~~~~~~~~~~~~~~~~~~~~~~~~~

but I do remember this: my father listened en
And then, with his usual quiet wisdom, he uttere
phrase to me that forever changed my life:

"The worst is over."

In that emotional moment, my disbelieving critical mind wanted to scream and ask him how he knew that. But I didn't do that. Because, in that moment, I could already feel the effect, like a healing balm flowing over my wounded soul.

It was Hope. Hope rising.

I decided to cling to Hope. In any case, I had nothing to lose, since my options were limited anyway.

My situation didn't immediately change after that conversation, but that conversation marked a clear turning point. My father was right: the worst was indeed over. Things started to get better because I started to get better. And I started to get better because I began to Hope.

One definition of Hope is this: "a person or thing that may help or save someone". (For e.g. "surgery is his only hope…"). Here is what I believe: Hope in itself is the thing that will help you or save you! In my opinion, if you can predict a positive outcome for something, then it's merely a prediction. But hope perseveres, even when prospects seem dim to the natural eye.

Hope involves surrender to God's will and His perfect plan for your life.

Hope believes that God is on your side, even if you created the mess in the first place.

Hope trusts that God will bring the best possible outcome to a situation. It may not be an outcome you expect or necessarily want, but in the fullness of time you will realize the beauty of God's plan, and you will see that it all worked together for your good. Even the very unpleasant things.

Hope enables you to quit moping and start living!

Hope empowers you to do the right thing. And to take steps that will propel you to victory.

It starts with Hope.

Are you going through a tough time? Then choose Hope!

**"The Lord himself will fight for you. Just stay calm." – Exodus 14:14 NLT**

**Aboa a ɔnni dua, Nyame na ɔpra ne ho.**
**It is the animal that has no tail that God brushes flies off. (God defends the defenseless) – Akan proverb**

~~~~~~~~~~~~~~~~~~~~~~~~~~

My personal experience of the Word of God is that it teaches me, soothes me and empowers me to make positive changes to my life. Recently, however, reading the Word of God also made me laugh out loud in mirth! I had been reading Psalm 3, written by David:
~~~~~~~~~~~~~~~~~~~~~~~~~~

"But You, O Lord, are a shield for me,
My glory and the One who lifts up my head.
I cried to the Lord with my voice, And He heard me from His holy hill. (Selah)
I lay down and slept; I awoke, for the Lord sustained me."

As I continued, I got to verse 7:

"Arise, O Lord; Save me, O my God! For You have struck all my enemies on the cheekbone..."

Huh? I thought that there had to be some Bible-fancy meaning to the phrase "[strike] all my enemies on the cheekbone," right? So, in my curiosity, I looked up a modern translation of that verse: "Arise, O Lord! Rescue me, my God! Slap all my enemies in the face!"

Upon reading that, I honestly could not help but burst out laughing. I pictured my 'enemy' walking down the street, being completely blindsided by a Powerful, Invisible Force giving them a THOROUGH air-slapping on my behalf!

Well, I couldn't tell you if that is exactly how God operates, but the verse served to remind me of some powerful truths:

- God is always looking out for me and protecting me
- God always has my back, even when the situation is dire or tragic

- When I call out to God, He answers
- God fights my battles

Therefore, I don't need to stress and strive unnecessarily! My job is to be the best *me* that God created me to be, with Him as my Rock, my Compass and my Guide as we navigate the sometimes-choppy waters of life together.

So, watch out, you enemies, frenemies, critics, backbiters and naysayers!! Watch out, powers, principalities and all spiritual enemies of my life!! Watch out, all you emotional enemies of defeat, despair and discouragement!!

Do you KNOW who I am? And most importantly, do you KNOW who my Father is??

Enemies, get out of my way and stop aggravating me!!! Or else, prepare to be (air or otherwise) SLAPPED in the face by my Father!!

Enemies, consider yourselves warned!!

## *Just Listen*

**"Too often we underestimate the power of a touch, a smile, a kind word, a listening ear, an honest compliment, or the smallest act of caring, all of which have the potential to turn a life around." – Leo Buscaglia**

**"When people talk, listen completely. Most people never listen." – Ernest Hemingway**

~~~~~~~~~~~~~~~~~~~~~~~~

My family and I immigrated to Connecticut, USA in the summer of 2001. Shortly thereafter, I began training for my new position as a pharmaceutical sales rep.

On September 11, 2001 I had a home study day and stayed in the library till mid-afternoon. Imagine my shock when I
~~~~~~~~~~~~~~~~~~~~~~~~

eventually heard the news of the tragedies that had taken place that day!

The following week, I started my new job. As the newest member of a high-performing, award-winning team, I felt enormous pressure to 'prove myself' and make good sales.

But as soon as I hit the field, I instinctively realized that I had to do my job differently in that season.

So, when I met with my physicians and their staff, I didn't go into hard selling. I began by simply asking, "How are you? How is your family?"

And I heard scores of personal stories! Many people had loved ones who lived in Connecticut and commuted to New York. Or they knew someone who did. EVERYBODY had a story.

And I would just listen.

I really came to appreciate the power of just listening. In hindsight, I see that it was a foreshadowing of my future career as a professional counselor.

Remarkably, my sales results were fantastic! I learned that, at the end of the day, people buy from people. When you truly care about the welfare of others, you WILL go far. And God WILL take care of your needs.

If, in the middle of a busy day, you come across someone who is having a hard day, do stop for a moment and take the time to ask them how they are doing.

And Just Listen.

I promise you, it will not be time wasted.

Purposeful Living

***"Obviously, I'm not trying to win the approval of people, but of God. If pleasing people were my goal, I would not be Christ's servant."– Galatians 1:10 NLT***

~~~~~~~~~~~~~~~~~~~~~~~~

Confession: I am a recovering people pleaser.

I have always considered myself to be a nice person, but I remember the first time I recognized that I also possessed an unhealthy need to gain the approval of others.

My husband was doing his residency training in Cambridge, United Kingdom. At the time, our son was about 6 months old. We lived in a community of flats that had been assigned to the resident physicians and their families.
~~~~~~~~~~~~~~~~~~~~~~~~

I quickly became friends with Dalal (not her real name), who was from Iran. Dalal's son was a couple of months younger than mine. We would take our babies for walks together, exchange advice on motherhood and occasionally babysit for each other.

Dalal was gorgeous and intelligent and I was flattered that, out of all the doctors' wives in our neighborhood, she had chosen me to be her neighborhood best friend.

One Saturday morning, Dalal knew I was going into town and she came to my door, asking if I would "please" get her a "few" groceries. I immediately agreed. But when she showed me her list, I realized that the list was much longer than I had anticipated. Worse, I was actually not even planning to go to the part of town where some of those items were sold.

I began to stammer my attempt to tell Dalal that her request was actually very inconvenient for me. But before I could finish my sentence, her list was in my hand. Dalal gave me a tight hug, told me how grateful she was to have a wonderful friend like me and in a poof, she was gone!

Dumbstruck, I put the list in my pocket. Dalal's request to buy her a "few" groceries took up nearly my whole afternoon. Later that evening, exhausted, I critically took stock of my friendship with her. To my dismay, it dawned on me that Dalal was the one constantly making requests, while

I felt like I was always bending over backwards to accommodate her.

Years later, I recognized, to my even greater dismay, that I had several other friendships not unlike my friendship with Dalal. And I was the common denominator.

Was it just my luck to have friends who took advantage of my friendship? Of course not! Two situations from my childhood proffered me some clues as to the roots of my behavior:

As the eldest child and grandchild in my family, I felt that there were high expectations of me and so I made it my mission early in life, to do 'nice' things that would gain me approval.

Secondly, my family moved a lot when I was growing up and I often found myself in the situation of being the new kid at a school, feeling completely out of my depth. Again, I discovered that being 'nice' helped me gain acceptance in my new environment.

My ever-ready willingness to accommodate people gained me their approval and admiration. But I would often put the needs of others before mine and as the years rolled by, I often found myself feeling overstretched and resentful.

I needed to change.

Don't get me wrong; I truly value being generous with my time and with my substance. But as I analyzed my behavior, I realized that I possessed definite traits of a people pleaser: difficulty saying *No* to people, taking on a task without really counting the impact it would have on me and on my family and then feeling resentful when I did so much for someone and yet they did not react in kind.

Here is what I realized:

- Being a people pleaser is NOT the same as being a kind person

- The most compassionate people do set boundaries! And because they are able to be kind and understanding to themselves, they are actually more able to be kind and understanding to others

- It is important to be kind to others, but it's equally important to be kind to myself

- I will never be able to please all the people all the time, so I won't even try. Bob Marley said that, and I agree

- I definitely cannot seek to please people AND be pleasing to God, so I won't try that either. St. Paul said that, and I agree

- Pleasing people is not my purpose in life. My purpose in life is to be pleasing to God and to accomplish whatever He has called me to do

- The older I get, the more I appreciate that my time and energy are finite. Therefore, I have decided to commit my time and energy to activities that are in line with God's plan and purpose for my life

- People who seem to like me solely because of what I do for them really do not care about me. My real friends love me for who I am

- It's not wrong to count the cost of an undertaking in terms of your time and resources *before* you commit to anything. When I do that, I'm much less likely to feel resentful

- I don't have to respond immediately to every request. It's my prerogative to tell people to give me time to think about it. And then, I can weigh all my options and preferences, before giving them a response

- Giving up people pleasing starts with a simple "No"

## One Talent Servant

*(a.k.a. the servant who allowed his fear to overshadow his purpose)*

“I can accept failure, everyone fails at something. But I can't accept not trying.” – Michael Jordan

“When I stand before God at the end of my life, I would hope that I would not have a single bit of talent left, and could say, 'I used everything you gave me.'” – Erma Bombeck

"For it will be like a man going on a journey, who called his servants and entrusted to them his property. To one he gave five talents, to another two, to another one, to each according to his ability. Then he went away. He who had received the five talents went at once and traded with them, and he made five talents more. So also he who had the two talents made two talents more.

But he who had received the one talent went and dug in the ground and hid his master's money. Now after a long time the master of those servants came and settled accounts with them. And he who had received the five talents came forward, bringing five talents more, saying, 'Master, you delivered to me five talents; here, I have made five talents more.' His master said to him, 'Well done, good and faithful servant. You have been faithful over a little; I will set you over much. Enter into the joy of your master.' And he also who had the two talents came forward, saying, 'Master, you delivered to me two talents; here, I have made two talents more.' His master said to him, 'Well done, good and faithful servant. You have been faithful over a little; I will set you over much. Enter into the joy of your master.' He also who had received the one talent came forward, saying, 'Master, I knew you to be a hard man, reaping where you did not sow, and gathering where you scattered no seed, so I was afraid, and I went and hid your talent in the ground. Here, you have what is yours.' But his master answered him, 'You wicked and slothful servant! You knew that I reap where I have not sown and gather where I scattered no seed? Then you ought to have invested my money with the bankers, and at my coming I should have received what was my own with interest. So take the talent from him and give it to him who has the ten talents. For to everyone who has will more be given, and he will have an abundance. But from

**the one who has not, even what he has will be taken away. And cast the worthless servant into the outer darkness. In that place there will be weeping and gnashing of teeth.'" – Matthew 25:14-30 (ESV) – The Parable of the Talents**

~~~~~~~~~~~~~~~~~~~~~~~~~~

The *Parable of the Talents* is a Bible story that intrigued me as a child. Specifically, it was the conclusion of the parable that confounded me. I had been taught in Sunday school that the Parable of the Talents was about stewardship, so I understood that the Master was displeased with the servant who had been entrusted with one talent, but who had failed to produce a profit from the talent. However, why was the Master so furious? Why did he punish One Talent Servant so severely?

One Talent Servant knew that his Master was a harsh man who did not suffer fools gladly. So, to him, the safest move was to bury the one talent in the ground. And upon the Master's return, he returned the talent back to the Master; uninvested, unspent and unused.

As a naturally risk-averse person, I could identify with One Talent Servant's reluctance to put the talent into an investment that could go bad. Plus, it wasn't as if One Talent Servant had brought back less than the one talent he had
~~~~~~~~~~~~~~~~~~~~~~~~~~

originally been given. So, for a time, I couldn't see what upset the Master so much.

Thankfully, age and wisdom eventually brought me new insight and a deeper understanding of the Master and One Talent Servant.

The Master made his servants stewards over his property, his wealth. This means that he expected them to develop, to invest, to work with, to manage, to maintain, to care for and/or to have oversight over the wealth they had been entrusted with, in order to increase its value. Therefore, each servant was expected to ***work*** – that is, ***to expend mental and physical effort*** – with the talents he had been given in order to make what they had been entrusted with more valuable.

So, being cognizant of the Master's expectation, why would One Talent Servant choose to do nothing? Here are a few possible reasons that came to my mind. (Disclaimer: this is MY interpretation of the motivations behind One Talent Servant's behavior.)

**DID HE FEAR FAILURE?**

One Talent Servant wanted to completely avoid the possibility of failing. He was afraid that if he failed to make a profit, the Master, who was a "hard man" (vs 24) would mete out a severe punishment onto him. So, he made the decision to bury the talent in the ground and do nothing further.

But this is what One Talent Servant needed to realize: making mistakes is part of the learning process! The choice is ours as to whether we will view a mistake as a soul-crushing failure, or as a learning opportunity, essential to the process of achieving proficiency and mastery.

Two pertinent definitions of the word 'failure' are as follows: "the omission of expected or required action" and "the action or state of not functioning"[1].

Making a mistake does not make a person a failure. Failure is when we waste the talents we were blessed with.

One of my favorite quotes is from Teddy Roosevelt's *Man in the Arena*: "It is not the critic who counts; nor the man who points out how the strong man stumbles, or where the doer of deeds could have done better. The credit belongs to the man who is actually in the arena... who strived valiantly; who errs, who comes again and again, because there is no effort with error and shortcoming...who at the best knows in the end the triumph of high achievement, and who at the worst, if he fails, at least fails while daring greatly."

## WAS HE STUCK IN HIS COMFORT ZONE?

A "comfort zone" describes the recurring, familiar, thoughts, attitudes and behaviors in our lives that bring low

[1]Failure. (2010), In The New Oxford American's Dictionary (3rd ed.). Oxford, UK: Oxford University Press

challenge, low risk, and low stress. We don't have any information about One Talent Servant prior to the Master's trip. Could it have been that the Master's expectations of One Talent Servant were outside of the areas of his knowledge and strengths and expertise, i.e. his comfort zone? And, therefore, could the uncertainty that One Talent Servant felt about this assignment have triggered an overabundance of caution and unwillingness to step out of his comfort zone? "Nothing ventured, nothing gained", as the saying goes; and that is exactly what happened to One Talent Servant.

## WAS HE STUCK IN THE PERFECTIONISM TRAP?

After the Master had distributed talents to the servants, the other two servants "went at once" and "traded" with their talents. But One Talent Servant did not. Was this possibly a clue that he suffered from the disease of perfectionism? One sign of perfectionism is the mindset of "if I can't do it perfectly, then I won't even try". Alternatively, One Talent Servant may have been procrastinating when the Master unexpectedly returned home from his journey. Procrastination is another sign of a perfectionist mindset. Perhaps One Talent Servant was waiting for the "perfect time" to begin? Here is the thing about waiting for a "perfect time" to begin to build your dream – there is no "perfect time" in life. And (s)he who keeps stalling may run out of time...

**WAS HE UNWILLING TO "DO THE TIME"?**

Bringing a dream into fruition CANNOT happen without effort, hard work, sacrifice, dedication, focus, resilience, consistency and courage. One Talent Servant displayed none of those qualities. Unsurprisingly he had nothing to show for the talent that had been given to him. He had put absolutely no effort into his assignment, not even to deposit the money into a bank where it could earn interest. His Master rightly called him "slothful'.

**DID HE FALL INTO THE COMPARISON TRAP?**

When the Master shared out the talents to his servants, he gave "to each according to his ability", and One Talent Servant received the least value of talents. Maybe that caused him to believe that he had less ability and therefore was less worthy than the other servants. Perhaps this belief led him to bury his talent in embarrassment, fearing that if the other servants discovered that he had only received one talent, they would mock him. But One Talent Servant failed to recognize a very important fact: the Master's expectations of him were EXACTLY in line with the size and nature of the specific talents that he had been given! He had everything he needed. The one talent he had been given was enough for him to accomplish what he was meant to accomplish, according to the Master's expectations. Secondly, comparing himself to the other servants rather than focusing on the talent he had been given could have caused One Talent Servant to look down on himself and lose sight of the fact that his one talent was actually of immense value! According to biblical scholar John R. Donovan, one talent in those days was worth 15 years' wages for an ordinary worker[2]. So a great responsibility had indeed been placed on One Talent Servant to develop his talent. Had Michael Jackson or Bob Marley or Isaac Newton or Stephen Hawking judged their worth based on the areas where they were not as talented as their peers, they would have failed to recognize and develop the amazing talents that they HAD been blessed with.

One Talent Servant blew his opportunity to do something amazing with his talent. By deciding to bury his talent in the ground and do nothing, he allowed fear to prevail. His life then became a portrait of inaction, apathy and laziness. No wonder his Master was so upset. One Talent Servant had let his Master down and, in doing so, he had let himself down as well.

[2]Siricoe, RA 1994 Talents: The Bible and Entrepreneurs, accessed January 31, 2020, <https://fee.org/articles/the-parable-of-the-talents-the-bible-and-entrepreneurs/>

# What Time Is It?

**"There is an appointed time for everything." – Ecclesiastes 3:1 NASB**

**"Everything comes to you at the right time. Be patient and trust the process." – Unknown**

**"Timing is everything in life and in golf." – Arnold Palmer**

~~~~~~~~~~~~~~~~~~~~~~~~~~

I had a conversation with a lady who had just gone through a devastating breakup.

She had had a difficult romantic history, and when this man came into her life, she was incredibly excited. He possessed all the qualities she desired in a mate. It seemed like he was
~~~~~~~~~~~~~~~~~~~~~~~~~~

the perfect guy for her. They fell passionately in love and very quickly they began to merge their lives together.

But the bliss of their new union did not last. It wasn't long before things began to unravel. There were a lot of control issues in their relationship and their arguments were heated and nasty.

The argument that led to their breakup did not seem like anything out of the ordinary. She had assumed, as with previous arguments, that it would blow over and life would eventually settle back to normal. But that argument was the straw that broke the camel's back. She was completely blindsided.

The shock and grief of the breakup hit her extremely hard. She felt pained that she had experienced such *bad luck* with men.

As we spoke, though, she came to the realization that a big part of what she was actually mourning was the loss of an ideal, to find the "perfect" guy and have the "perfect" relationship. She had mistakenly thought she had found the perfect guy, and the truth, as she came to realize, was that their relationship had been FAR from perfect.

Not only was it time for her to face this reality, but it was also time for her to take ownership of the role she had been playing in propagating their unhealthy relationship.

In short, she realized that there were areas of her life where she needed to heal, areas where she needed to grow, and wisdom she needed to acquire.

Without addressing those areas, she realized that she is likely to find herself in yet another relationship with the SAME unhealthy patterns.

Her breakthrough came in the realization that it was time for her to begin to deal with some of her lifelong issues.

As for the future of that relationship, who knows? Perhaps they will one day find themselves back in each other's arms. Or perhaps not.

But her happiness, moving forward, will depend on whether she uses this newly single season of her life to heal and grow and rebuild.

Conversely, she could fail to appreciate the significance of this season of her life, blame "bad luck with men" for her problems and jump into the next relationship, hoping that this time she will hit the "perfect guy" jackpot.

Nature operates in seasons. Spring is usually the optimal time for planting, and autumn, for harvest. Many fruits and plants are seasonal; if planted in the right season, a plant grows best and gives its best yield.

If planted in the wrong season, plants fail to thrive.

Our lives also operate in seasons. Throughout birth to childhood, teen years and adulthood, there are seasonal activities and tasks and lessons that we must learn and master. Only then do we successfully move on to the next phase of our lives.

Our lives become complicated when we fail to learn the lessons from previous seasons. However, life does bring us the opportunity to learn those lessons. I call them the 'Rewind & Repair Seasons'. They are built into the cycle of our lives.

In the 'Rewind & Repair Seasons', we may have to backtrack a bit. We may have to unlearn bad habits. And learn new healthy habits. In this season, we may have to modify or even discontinue certain relationships.

It can be a scary time. But it is important to believe that all things WILL work out for our good in the long run.

Just stay the course of the season of your life. Pay attention to the lessons that life is trying to teach you in that particular time and season.

Life flows when we understand and honor the seasons of our lives. Otherwise, we will find ourselves stuck in the same frustrating cycles of issues we have not addressed.

The Bible says that there is a season to everything and a time for every activity in this life. Some examples from Ecclesiastes 3:

A time to plant and a time to harvest...

A time to tear down and a time to build up...

A time to scatter stones and a time to gather stones...

A time to search and a time to quit searching...

A time to tear and a time to mend...

A time to be quiet and a time to speak...

Do you really know what season of your life you are in? One good question to ask yourself today is this: *What time is it?*

## *Semicolon;*

**"… and hope does not disappoint." – Romans 5:5 NASB**

**"I will not die; instead I will live…" – Psalms 118:17 NLT**

**"All shall be well, and all shall be well and all manner of thing shall be well." – Julian of Norwich**

**"He said not 'Thou shalt not be tempested, thou shalt not be travailed, thou shalt not be dis-eased'; but he said, 'Thou shalt not be overcome." – Julian of Norwich**

~~~~~~~~~~~~~~~~~~~~~~~~~

To look at her, one would never have guessed what she had been through. She was strikingly beautiful and carried
~~~~~~~~~~~~~~~~~~~~~~~~~

herself with confident ease and a winning smile as she worked her way through the crowd at the event. Nothing in her pedigree, nor in the personal and professional accomplishments listed on her resume suggested that she had led anything but a charmed, privileged, accomplished life.

She walked over to me, introduced herself and then stretched her hand out to me in a friendly handshake. That was when I spotted the small symbol tattooed on the inside of her right wrist. Curious, I looked closer and noticed that it was a symbol of a semicolon.

My interest piqued, I blurted, "What's that symbol on your wrist?". As soon as I spoke, I regretted my forwardness and began to apologize. But she put me at ease and reassured me that it was all right. Then she explained the symbolism behind her semicolon tattoo, and went on to share her story of being a suicide survivor…

~~~~~~~~~~~~~~~~~~~~~~~~~~

A semicolon is a punctuation mark (;) indicating a pause. A semicolon connects two clauses or two sentences. According to The Semicolon Project: "A semicolon is used when an author could have chosen to end their sentence, but chose not to. The author is you and the sentence is your life. The semicolon is symbolic of our lives and how we have chosen
~~~~~~~~~~~~~~~~~~~~~~~~~~

to carry on. Your story is not over". (Ref: The Semicolon Project)[3]

I was blown away by this simple yet incredibly powerful concept of the semicolon. And, to me, the power in the symbolism of the semicolon extends even beyond the critical decision to refuse to end one's life. There are many people who, although they may not have physically attempted suicide, essentially stopped living. They allowed themselves to 'die' inside, even though their physical bodies are still alive.

The semicolon signals that the writer is not done; the writer plans to continue writing the sentence, beyond the semicolon pause. What the sentence will say after the semicolon is completely up to the writer. And so, to me, the semicolon symbolically heralds the critical point in our lives following a crisis. This is the point where we have to make a decision as to which direction our lives will go. At that point, to shield ourselves from further hurt and disappointment, the easier option might be to stop living and loving. Or, it can be the point at which we make the decision to pause, reflect and regroup. And then, armed with new wisdom, and a renewed faith, we will choose to continue with the business of living life to the full.

[3]The Semicolon Project is a mental health advocacy group of people dedicated to the prevention of suicide.

It is a given, that in this life, we may experience failure, disappointment, discouragement, disparagement, shattered dreams, frustrations, betrayals, debilitating illnesses, tough financial times or any combination of these. These challenges may come even when we do the right thing and even though we are walking in God's Will for our lives. Any of these challenges has the power to plunge us into the utter depths of despair; where we no longer want to engage in life, take risks or put ourselves out there for the good of anyone or any cause. Because all we want to do is to wrap ourselves in cotton wool and insulate ourselves from the possibility of getting hurt again.

I've been there. I've been tempted to do just that. But, what I know for sure is that God has a unique purpose for my life. And what I also know is that achieving my purpose doesn't come without travail. Furthermore, I know that life is meant to be lived fully.

So, in those moments when setbacks have me tempted to pack it in and place a 'full stop' on my efforts or on living my life to the full, I remind myself that my story is not over; I have the option to insert a semicolon at that spot.

The semicolon reminds me that I don't have to give up on myself or on my life! Why? Because I have other options!

The semicolon prompts me to pause, reflect, regroup, and then continue writing the story that I was brought to this world to write. The setback I suffered was a twist in the tale that will serve to make the story of my life more engaging and impactful.

When I figuratively place a semicolon in my life, I literally pause; to rest, reflect, regroup and acquire new knowledge and a renewed determination. I now consider those semicolon moments of my life as pit stops where I PAUSE; to refuel my soul and rebuild my hope.

Taking the time to pause in life is of utmost importance. Taking the time to pause is a non-negotiable point in the recovery process. There are always important lessons that God wants me to learn from every situation. During the pause, I ask myself this critical question: HOW WILL THIS SITUATION MAKE ME A BETTER PERSON?

Secondly, as a faith-filled person, I believe that "All things work together for good…" (Romans 8:28). And, so, my next challenge is this: to find the good in that situation and hold on to it like my life depends on it. And my life does depend on it!

I also remind myself of these truths:

- The purpose for my life is bigger than the discouragement I'm facing in this moment.

- The dream I have been given by God is meant to be difficult by His design. Part of God's plan is to make me learn to rely on His Power that is at work in my life.

- What doesn't kill me will make me stronger.
- My purpose stems from God's Plan for my life. I am determined to complete His assignment on my life.

- I dare to believe that all things are possible because I believe in Him and trust Him.

- "I can't" is not in my vocabulary. I can do all things through Christ who strengthens me (Philippians 4:13 NKJV)

- This is a temporary setback. There are important lessons that God wants me to learn from this situation, and then I can move on.

- I am regrouping. I will not quit on God. And I will not quit on myself.

- God has given me grace to carry on.

- God will not leave me or forsake me.

- The Lord is the strength of my life; therefore I will not be afraid.

- No retreat, no surrender because I am an Overcomer.

- I am resilient. I will carry on!

**"Therefore I do not run like one who runs aimlessly or box like one beating the air." – 1 Corinthians 9:26 HCSB**

**"Don't set your own goals by what other people make important." – Lolly Daskal**

**"We must all suffer from one of two pains: the pain of discipline or the pain of regret. The difference is discipline weighs ounces while regret weighs tons." – Jim Rohn**

~~~~~~~~~~~~~~~~~~~~~~~~~~

One year, I really impressed myself with my goal-setting process. I set goals that were measurable, specific and concrete. I crafted my Personal Mission Statement. And then I laid out my goals and plans onto a phenomenal looking vision board. But, sadly, there were several important goals that I did not achieve that year.
~~~~~~~~~~~~~~~~~~~~~~~~~~

I decided not to beat myself up about it. However, to be accountable to myself, I still wanted to figure out why that happened. What had kept me from diligently pursuing and accomplishing my goals that year?

Let me pause here to re-introduce myself. My name is Aba and I am a Superwoman-oholic.

I confess that I am seduced by the illusion of a Superwoman who seems to have it ALL and do it ALL, ALL the time.

Is Superwoman even real? Or is she merely the elusive quest of perfectionism; fueling the insatiable need in us to keep doing more, yet ultimately causing us dissatisfaction and discontentment?

I don't know all the answers to the above, but here is what I realized about myself:

My energy is finite
There are only 24 hours in a day
Therefore I simply cannot do it all and be all, all the time

When a person makes a choice or decides on a specific course of action, they are effectively giving up other options. That is my layman's understanding of the theory of Opportunity Cost.

It's not necessarily hard to figure out our life's calling and the goals we need to set to help us achieve them. However, it's important to also be aware that our time and energy are limited resources. Therefore, an important consideration in this process lies in strategically answering this question: WHAT AM I WILLING TO GIVE UP IN ORDER TO WALK IN MY LIFE'S PURPOSE?

So, in addition to writing a *To Do* list of goals, it's equally important to create a *To Don't* list.

We were never supposed to do it all!

Philippians 4:13 NIV says, "I can do all this through Him who gives me strength".. However, without a fuller understanding of that verse, it's easy to be fooled into thinking that you are supposed to be God's 'do-all' Superman or Superwoman.

The Amplified version of that verse says this (emphasis mine): "I can do all things [WHICH HE HAS CALLED ME TO DO] through Him who strengthens and empowers me [TO FULFILL HIS PURPOSE...]". Philippians 4:13 AMP

So, first of all, it's important to figure out the things that God HAS CALLED ME TO DO, TO FULFILL HIS PURPOSE. It is those things for which God strengthens and empowers us!

Additional tasks we take on, nice or noble as they may be, will consume our energy and time and, ultimately, detract us from achieving God's purpose for our lives.

This year, as I am preparing my New Year's resolutions and goals, I will also make my "To Don't" list for the coming year.

What goes into a "To Don't" list?

Answer: the things we intend to give up or to stop doing so that we can free up our energy and time to accomplish our life's purposes.

Record in your "To Don't" list the toxic relationship you plan to separate yourself from. And, perhaps, your decision to forego 15 minutes of sleep everyday to give yourself time to pray and meditate in the mornings. Include your tactical intention to put away your smart phone in the evenings so that, instead of being tempted to mindlessly browse on social media, you can channel the time into studying. Or maybe your plan is to stop buying food from outside and, instead, start making your own lunch so that you can use the money you save to hire a personal trainer. Or your choice might be to stop spending all day on Saturday cleaning your house and instead hire a cleaner so that you can free up time to bond with your family.

Your "To Don't" list is just as important as your "To Do" goal list. Be strategic about creating both lists!

# *Reblocking*

**"The Lord had said to Abram, "Leave...I will bless you." – Genesis 12:1,2 NLT**

**"Change is the only constant in life" – Heraclitus, Greek Philosopher**

**"Change is inevitable. Growth is optional." – John Maxwell**

~~~~~~~~~~~~~~~~~~~~~~~~

Our crowd erupted into a loud cheer as their number was announced. We expected to see our girls immediately mount the stage; walking military-like in unison, graceful as swans. But, after an extended moment, they still hadn't appeared. After another eternity-filled pause, the announcer called for the next team in the lineup to perform.
~~~~~~~~~~~~~~~~~~~~~~~~

The other team moms and I exchanged startled glances as we whispered, "What happened?" to each other in confusion.

My teenage daughter is a youth competitive dancer. Competitive dance is a demanding sport that requires a high level of technical precision, artistry, stamina, discipline, versatility, strategy, teamwork and above all, a gladiator spirit.

Each team dance number is carefully choreographed down to the smallest detail. This process is called "blocking". The team practices the number over and over, till each dancer becomes completely familiar with the choreography as well as with their positioning on the stage during the dance.

But when a team member in a group dance is suddenly unable to perform, often due to unforeseen circumstances like sickness or injury, an empty spot in the dance is created where the team member should have been positioned. In such situations, it becomes necessary to "reblock" the dance to fill in the 'hole' created by the absent dancer.

My daughter says that the process of reblocking can feel awkward at first. The reason is that the dancers would have practiced a particular format and flow of a dance to the degree that it becomes ingrained and therefore making a change can feel challenging. Quoting my daughter Elissa, "You are so used to that other person's position in the dance, and how you dance your part relative to their position, that it becomes almost like muscle memory." Successful reblocking starts with 1) understanding that because there has been a change to the team makeup, the configuration of the dance must also change, and 2) deliberately setting out to make changes to the choreography to account for this new reality.

Reblocking sometimes must be done in the midst of trying circumstances; when emotions are high and team members are feeling blindsided. One of Elissa's teammates took ill the moment before the team was due on stage. But they quickly realized that they had to stay positive. So, they gathered their wits, informed the competition organizers about the situation and requested additional time to adjust to that unexpected development.

A ten-minute window was allotted to the girls. And they did it! They maintained their composure, stayed positive, successfully reblocked the dance and then went back on stage, giving it their all. They achieved excellent scores and our total admiration!

Reflecting on that moment, it dawned on me that, in life, we also encounter situations that make it necessary for us to reblock. In the course of our lives all of us will experience loss. Death of a loved one, divorces, breakups, relocations, job changes, friendships ending and children growing up and leaving home, are some instances.

Losing someone or something significant to our lives can leave us with an acute sense of heartbreak and imbalance. It is well known that we should give ourselves the opportunity to grieve our loss. What we are less prepared for is how pervasive grief can feel and how long grief can last. Often, even though we know we need to move on, we feel unable to take the next step.

There is a reason why we feel stuck in our grief. Grieving can be a complex experience because, not only do we miss the essence of the person we lost; we also miss them in all the various ways they were significant to our lives. The loss of the person we loved doesn't just leave one hole in our lives; it leaves several holes. And so reblocking must be done to fill all of those holes.

When my mother died, I didn't just lose a mother's love; I also lost my friend, my confidante, my mentor and my prayer warrior. My mother had been significant to my life in so many ways. And though I knew that I could never replace her, I still had to reblock my life to fill those holes that had been created so that I could move on from my crippling grief.

Relocating is a life event that can bring major upheaval in our lives. I have had to relocate many times in my life. Every time I moved to a different city or country, the change I experienced was so much more than just a change in my physical location and my job. Holes had been created in my life because of the loss of my church family, my social circle and my personal and professional support system. I had to reblock to fill those holes so that I could finally feel settled.

When the seasons in our lives change, it can bring us to a point where we no longer feel sure about who we are or what our purpose is in life; leading to an identity crisis. Another situation that can trigger an identity crisis is when we discover that a story about our life, which we had believed as truth, was actually a lie. Or when we come to the stark realization that our long-held views about life are out of place in today's world and no longer serve us well. In all of these situations, it becomes necessary to undertake a process of reblocking by changing our mindsets and gaining a new understanding and discovery of who we really are.

Reblocking, in the sense that I am using it, is the process of:

1) understanding that something has changed in our lives,
2) accepting that we must now also change,
3) identifying the holes that were created by this change, and
4) filling those holes.

Time, in and of itself, does not fill the holes. This is a process that must be done with intentionality. The reblocking process is the key that allows us to move forward successfully.

The term "reblocking" may be unfamiliar to you. But whatever you call it, know that during the course of our lives, we all reach points where life hits us with a curveball. When that happens, rather than resist this reality, we must embrace the change. And then, with intention, navigate our way through it.

Change is part of life, and therefore resisting change is not only futile, but can leave us feeling depressed, stagnant and stuck. For sure, change can be uncomfortable, but we can be encouraged in knowing that change opens our lives up to new and infinite possibilities.

And through all the changing scenes of our lives we must never forget this: God never changes! He will be with us through every change! He is our Help through every transition! What blindsided you did not blindside God, because nothing happens behind God's back! God knows what He is doing! His plans are to take care of us and to settle us in a good place in our lives!

*"Each step I take, You make a way…*
*My seasons change, You stay the same.*
*You're the God of all my days"*
*(From "God of All My Days" by Casting Crowns)*

## Stupid Thrones

"I applied my mind to study and to explore by wisdom all that is done under the heavens. What a heavy burden God has laid on mankind! I have seen all the things that are done under the sun; all of them are meaningless, a chasing after the wind." – Ecclesiastes 1:13-14 NIV

"What keeps us stuck and forever languishing in the muck and mire of whatever situation we're in is the utterly convincing but entirely false belief that there's nothing in our situation that we can do other than be stuck. Therefore, what's got us stuck in this mess has nothing to do with our situation, but everything to do with our belief about our situation." – Craig D. Lounsbrough

~~~~~~~~~~~~~~~~~~~~~~~~~~
~~~~~~~~~~~~~~~~~~~~~~~~~~

At age 7, I was a precocious child and an avid reader. To keep me occupied, my parents made sure I had a wide variety of reading material. Included in my collection was a book of stories adapted from Greek and Roman mythology. One of those stories was about a man called Damocles.

Disclaimer: When I researched the story of Damocles many years later, I realized that what I had read as a child had either presented a different version of the Damocles' story, or perhaps I had misunderstood certain details of that story. However, since I no longer have that book to reference, I may never know.

This is *my* version of the story of Damocles...

There was a king called Damocles, who was blessed with many riches. But Damocles had a problem. Directly above his throne was a huge sword hanging by a thin, fraying piece of leather nailed to the wall. The leather was stretched so thin that it looked like it would snap at any minute, which would then cause the sword to fall and strike Damocles on the head, instantly killing him.

Every day, King Damocles would sit on his magnificent throne; in splendor, yet terrified at the knowledge that the sword could fall on his head at any moment

Seven-year-old me could not understand why *'my'* Damocles daily chose to sit on that throne, underneath that sword; daily putting his life at risk, petrified that he would be killed.

After all, wasn't Damocles the king? Would shifting his throne a few inches, or choosing to sit in a different seat altogether, have changed his royal status?

It's easy to spot the folly in *my* Damocles' story. But in reality, how many of us, just like *my* Damocles, allow ourselves to stay mired in situations and circumstances that are potentially detrimental to our physical, spiritual and emotional well being?

***Chasing after the wind...***

*My* Damocles' viewed his throne as a status symbol, not unlike how society today views status symbols as a proxy for wealth. But is our worth determined by the clothes we wear or the cars we drive or the houses we live in? Our misplaced value system has created an insatiable need in us to acquire material possessions.

And to what end? Many of us live above our means, gathering debt and enslaving ourselves to the rat race. Some risk their health to acquire more material possessions, while others are willing to compromise their integrity for this quest. King Solomon, the writer of Ecclesiastes called it "meaningless, a chasing after the wind" (Ecclesiastes 1:14). Breaking out of this pointless cycle starts with taking stock of what really matters in your life.

***What has you stuck?***

*My* Damocles was attached to the splendor of his throne while terrified everyday that the dangling sword would fall upon his head. What an unnecessary and unwise way to live!

Certain choices do not make us courageous; they are just stupid. Yet that is how many of us choose to live. These stupid thrones and dangling swords can wreck us, if we don't change! The process of change starts with a fearless self-inventory.

***Food for thought***

*What stupid thrones are we choosing to sit on every day?* Regret? Refusal to adapt to changing circumstances in our lives? The need to look perfect or prosperous?

*What swords are we allowing to dangle above our heads?* Unforgiveness? Ruthless ambition? Addictions?

P.S. If you were curious enough to read up on the story of Damocles, you will know by now how vastly different my childhood interpretation of the story was from the original version!

**"But when He, the Spirit of truth comes, He will guide you into all truth." – John 16:13 NASB**

**"Whether you turn to the right or to the left, your ears will hear a voice behind you, saying, 'This is the way; walk in it.'" – Isaiah 30:21 NIV**

~~~~~~~~~~~~~~~~~~~~~~~~~~

I once spent a small fortune getting a problem on my car fixed. When the car still didn't sound right, and the service agent was slow to respond to my calls, I was vexed. By the time I got a hold of him on the phone, I was sorely tempted to give him a strong piece of my mind. But at that moment, on the phone, a feeling that was almost palpable cautioned me to refrain from being aggressive or impatient with the service agent.
~~~~~~~~~~~~~~~~~~~~~~~~~~

Boy, was I glad I obeyed. When I arrived at the dealership thirty minutes after our phone conversation, that service agent had passed out at his desk, hit his head and was lying unconscious on the floor with his concerned colleagues standing around him. Apparently he had complained of chest pains that day.

I watched in shock as paramedics rushed him to the hospital...

Some people may call it intuition. I call it being led by the Spirit of God.

Being led by the Spirit of God may not make sense to us in that moment because we are often limited by what our five senses can perceive and because we have incomplete information about a situation.

But God, who knows all things, knows the end from the beginning. In the fullness of time, all will be revealed. And we will be left with awe and gratitude that we listened to Him!

How can we be better equipped to pick out the voice of God from the other influences in our lives? Let's invest a few minutes every day to read the Word of God. Let's ask God everyday to be our guide.

That's a start.

# Some Have Entertained Angels

**"Do not neglect to show hospitality to strangers, for by this some have entertained angels without knowing it." – Hebrews 13:2 NASB**

**"When we gather together in the moonlit village ground it is not because of the moon. Every man can see it in his own compound. We come together because it is good for kinsmen to do so." – Chinua Achebe's *Things Fall Apart***

~~~~~~~~~~~~~~~~~~~~~~~~~~~

Entertaining was a common feature in our home growing up, because my father was a career diplomat.

It seemed to me – especially in the periods where he was on a posting abroad – that we had guests over for dinner at least once a week; often a Ghanaian government official or
~~~~~~~~~~~~~~~~~~~~~~~~~~~

delegation. My father would quite often spontaneously invite people, so my mother perfected the art of putting together a simple, elegant meal at little notice.

Also – if I am not exaggerating – it seemed to me that we had visitors stay over at our house at least once a month. These guests would typically be personal friends of my parents who were traveling for work. Staying at our home meant that they could save on hotel and meal costs. Because of that, we had a guest room that was always ready to welcome the next guest.

Looking back, it doesn't surprise me that this was our lifestyle. Both of my parents naturally had warm and inviting personalities and they were incredibly generous in their hospitality. Their motives were purely to extend goodwill; to give people a sense of home, when they were away from home.

Hospitality – the friendly and generous reception and entertainment of guests – was such a part of the rhythm of our everyday lives, that I grew up assuming that it was the norm in every household. And as I got older, I realized that I had definitely inherited the hospitality "gene". In fact, my husband Eddie likes to tell this funny story from our wedding. I had selected a 12-place setting china for our wedding gift registry. When he asked me why we needed all those place settings, I responded incredulously "to entertain, of course!", upon which he, even more incredulously, asked me, "Who do you think I am, your father?!". At the time

Eddie was doing his medical residency in the United Kingdom and lived in a small apartment in a complex that the hospital had designated to house doctors.

But as a young adult still living at home with my parents, I too began to occasionally invite my friends over for weekend stays at our home. At the time I was a graduate student at Queen's University in Kingston, Ontario Canada.

Queen's was a wonderful experience for me. I made a lot of friends, many of them international students like myself. I recognized, though, that I was in a uniquely fortunate position because my family lived only an hour and half away by car. Most of the other international students did not have that luxury.

At that time, my father served as Ghana's envoy to Canada, so home for us was the Ghana High Commissioner's residence, located in scenic Rockcliffe Park, Ottawa. The residence was a stately home, purpose built for entertaining, yet with intimate touches added by my mother to exude a warm, inviting family atmosphere. It had a huge yard in the back that boasted an array of maple, birch and oak trees that glistened with snow in the winter and was majestic with red, orange and yellow splendor in the fall.

Over the course of my two years at Queen's (1993 through to 1995), I made it a point to invite my friends, especially the international students, home to spend weekends in Ottawa with my family and me. Like my parents, I too wanted to give them a little bit of home away from home, I suppose. And, so, the friends I brought home for the weekend were from Hong Kong, Mauritius, India, Singapore, Japan, China, Nigeria, Kenya, Canada and, of course, Ghana.

I very much enjoyed meeting Ghanaian students. Having lived the majority of my formative years outside Ghana, I seized the opportunity to get to know other young Ghanaians. In particular, I made several friends from Ghana who were in the Master of Laws (LLM) program at Queen's. It had been a tradition of sorts for Queen's University to admit students from the University of Ghana Law School and quite a number of eminent Ghanaian lawyers had the opportunity to pursue that program.

The weekends we spent at my home were low-key; nothing spectacular. There was usually lots of laughter and conversation with my family around the dinner table, a little sightseeing and then it was back to school on Sunday afternoon.

Almost three decades later, I am still in contact with many of these people and feel honored to still count some of them as my friends. I feel proud to know that many of them have gone on to lead successful and influential lives. Of course, when I formed those connections I didn't know that. I became friends with them because they were intelligent people with great personalities. In hindsight, I can see the greatness that was in them; although back then, I wasn't so aware of it.

The first Ghanaian friend I met when I started at Queen's was an LLM student who was halfway through his program. He was bright, eloquent, had a witty sense of humor and was also an accomplished musician. As broke students, we became movie-watching buddies on the half-priced movie night Tuesdays. The weekend I brought him home, we all went down to the basement after dinner and sang songs while he strummed along with his guitar. We lost touch a couple of years after we left Queen's and reconnected about 15 years later on Facebook. That is when I realized that my friend Ace Ankomah had become one of Ghana's premier lawyers and a prominent political activist.

In my second year at Queen's, I became friends with another Ghanaian international student pursuing the LLM. I felt very comfortable with Charlotte right from the first conversation I had with her. She was beautiful, a great conversationalist and had a sincerity and a directness about her that I really appreciated. I also liked the fact that, though she was clearly brilliant, she was approachable and positive. I always enjoyed spending time with Charlotte.

The weekend I invited Charlotte over to Ottawa had been spontaneous, as I recall. Charlotte accepted my invitation and then asked if she could bring a friend along; another Ghanaian who had just started the LLM program. Her friend's name was Julia. Although Julia and I had not met, we had several mutual friends and I had seen her on campus when we were both in undergrad at the University of Ghana. Julia was striking to look at, with gorgeous doe eyes. She was more reserved, but very pleasant. Before long, Charlotte had put us both at ease and we chatted like old friends on a whole range of topics.

We had a great weekend. I clearly remember, during that weekend, looking at Julia and trying to come up with an adjective to describe her, but the word eluded me. Some days later, though, the word I had been looking for came to me. It was "Regal".

My friend Charlotte is now Mrs. Charlotte Osei, the UN International Elections Commissioner, an eminent lawyer and former chairperson of the Electoral Commission of Ghana.

Julia became Lady Julia Osei Tutu, wife of Asantehene, Otumfuo Nana Osei Tutu II, monarch of the Ashanti kingdom.

These are just three profiles of many wonderful people that I met at Queen's. I had just been extending hospitality, one weekend at a time.

How was I to have known the greatness that had crossed my path?

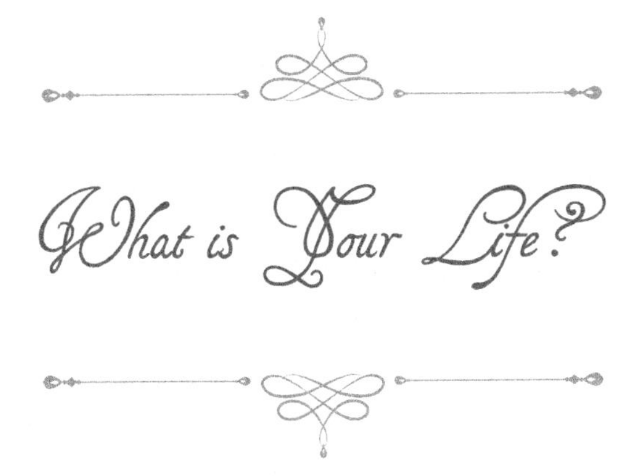
What is Your Life?

## *Vapor-Life*

**"For what is your life? It is even a vapor that appears for a little time and then vanishes away." – James 4:14 NKJV**

**"The greatest tragedy in life is not death, but a life without a purpose." – Dr. Myles Munroe**

~~~~~~~~~~~~~~~~~~~~~~~~~~

Reading *The Purpose Driven Life* changed my life two decades ago. My take away message was that God created me for a specific purpose and that in turn, I am charged with figuring out and accomplishing the specific plans for which God placed me on this earth.

Armed with that mindset, I launched into my thirties with a fervency and a fear.
~~~~~~~~~~~~~~~~~~~~~~~~~~

My fervency? To achieve something great. To have my big moment. To hit my major life crescendo that would leave an indelible mark on this world for God and for humanity.

My fear? That I would not be able to accomplish my life tasks. Or that I would run out of time before I could achieve something great enough or remarkable enough or bequeathable enough to leave behind for the next generations.

Having recently hit my mid-century mark, I am more aware than ever about my mortality. And I admit that there have been many times over the past decade that I have feared that I was running out of time. I'm not trying to be morbid, but the reality is that at 50 years of age, there are likely more years behind me than in front of me. The Bible says, "As for the days of our lives, they contain seventy years. Or, if due to strength, eighty years," (Psalms 90:10 NASB). And yet there is so much that I still want to accomplish in this life!

I am particularly sorrowful when I hear about the death of a young person. It is sad to think that somebody's life was cut short. Yet I have been witness to the stories of people who lived very brief lives on this earth, but still managed to make their mark. I have also seen young people whose light burned so brightly that they set the world on fire at a tender age and then continued to live long, meaningful, impactful lives.

I have seen people who lived longer than three score and ten years on this earth but died with so much unrealized potential. And I have seen others who had a slow start in life, but who, like a fine wine that ages to perfection, grew beautifully to accomplish their divine purpose in life.

My conclusion, therefore, is that a person's impact is not necessarily dependent on the chronological years they are given. Everybody is different.

The truth, as I believe it to be, is that the amount of time we get to live on this earth is predetermined by God. "All the days ordained for me were written in your book before one of them came to be." – Psalm 139:16 AMP

The time we are given on this earth is not up to us, it's up to God. Don't misunderstand me, it's still our job to look after our physical, spiritual and mental health so that we can live healthy, productive, joyful, fulfilling lives – according to the days that were ORDAINED for us.

People are given different life spans on this earth-realm; that is just the way it is. But what I have realized is that, regardless of how many years a person lives on earth – whether 0 or 130 years – all of our lives are like vapor compared to the length of eternity.

According to God's eternal perspective, one day for God is like a thousand years for us on earth (2 Peter 3:8). I'm not a Bible scholar, but just to give myself a sense of perspective, I did the math on that ratio. I realized that according to that biblical ratio, if a person lives to be 80 years old, then, according to God's perspective, his lifespan is less than two hours!

Life is indeed a vapor! Therefore, the big question and the divine task for each of us, however long the life we are granted on this earth realm is, remains the same: *How am I going to live out this my vapor-life to serve humanity to the glory of God?*

Our truth? None of us has much time!

## I Was Here

**"Please think about your legacy because you are writing it every day." – Gary Vaynerchuk**

**"Now finish the work, so that you may complete it just as eagerly as you began, according to your means. For if the willingness is there, the gift is acceptable according to what one has, not according to what one does not have." – 2 Corinthians 8:11,12 BSB**

~~~~~~~~~~~~~~~~~~~~~~~~~

July 6, 2019: the news outlets have been saturated with reports about the death of a 20-year-old actor. He had been well loved in our household, because my daughter had grown up watching him on the Disney channel. The reports stated that he died of epilepsy.
~~~~~~~~~~~~~~~~~~~~~~~~~

As I continued reading the reports, my mind wasn't so much on the young man's death, but on his remarkable life. He had not let his medical condition stop him from achieving notable success as an actor. Beyond that, he had used his celebrity status to support and create awareness for several worthy humanitarian causes.

I was very inspired by a statement he had made several months before his death: *"We all go…what you leave behind should be bigger than you"*.

How did this young man, with money in his pocket and success under his belt, working in an industry where the pitfalls of excessive, self-indulgent living are all too real, manage to leave such a legacy in his short life?

I observed several important principles in him that I believe are critical if one is to lead a meaningful life:

- Follows God's will
- Goes beyond a self-absorbed existence of eat, sleep, work, play; repeat
- Serves humanity through giving of one's time, money,
- influence or talents
- Touches lives in a positive way
- And, therefore, leaves a legacy

My great desire is to leave this earth knowing that I achieved all that I was supposed to achieve, and that in doing so, I impacted lives in a memorable way and left the world a better place. And I want people to know that I did this to glorify God.

But, with all my best intentions, there were constantly things in my life that seemed to sabotage my attempts to be my best self. The challenges in my life. My character flaws. My mistakes and missteps. And the cycles of guilt, fear, self-doubt and negative self-talk.

I would get very discouraged thinking that the problem was me, till I came to the realization that the problem actually lay in three lies I had believed about life.

*Lie #1: To live a meaningful life, your life has to be perfectly put together*

The truth is that no one's life is perfect. Everybody is fighting a battle in their lives. And using the concept of a path as a metaphor for life, no one's path flows smoothly all the way through their life. As we journey through life, we will experience sections of our path that are winding and steep and lonely and rocky and filled with thorns. These represent the difficult seasons of our lives where pain, sickness, sadness, mistakes, regrets, betrayals, disappointments, grief, divorce, brokenness and trauma find us. We may even be tempted to give up on the journey because the burdens are so great.

But whoever promised us a pain-free, problem-free, challenge-free life? What God did promise was that He would walk with us through our problems. And the truth, as I have come to know it, is that it is actually during the difficult seasons of our lives that we gain wisdom and resilience, build up faith, discover new purpose for our lives and develop the ability to be joyful as we await the breakthrough.

What I have also learned about life is that we often encounter challenges in the areas where we are gifted and called to make a difference to the world. My friend Ajoa is an extremely talented hair stylist. But what truly sets Ajoa apart is her God-given gift of speaking life into her clients. People leave Ajoa's salon not only looking beautiful, but also feeling encouraged and empowered. Ajoa continues to be an excellent hair stylist and motivator despite the fact that she suffers from chronic pain in her right hand as a result of an injury she sustained in a car accident some years ago.

Furthermore, I have seen that the opportunities we are given to live meaningful and purpose-filled lives arise just as much out of our challenges, as they do because of our gifts and talents. One example that always comes to my mind is the TV show, "America's Most Wanted". During the twenty-five seasons that the show aired, thousands of child abductors were caught and brought to justice. The executive producer of that show was John Walsh, whose own son was kidnapped and murdered in 1981. Out of John's greatest pain came great purpose. God's purposes are often accomplished in our lives through tough situations.

*Lie #2: To live a meaningful life, you have to be perfectly put together*

The truth is that I am a work in progress. And, I've come to realize, it's not about perfection. God never used anyone because they were perfect. What God wants is a heart that is willing to be used by Him. It is, and always has been, about the heart.

My job is to cling to the truth of who God is and the truth of who God says I am. I am the beloved child of God.

My job is to I trust that God is fulfilling His purpose in my life and to know that He is the God who is able to take the broken pieces of my life and mold me into something beautiful, for His Glory.

Even when my prayers have seemingly been denied and it appears as if my dream has been squashed, I will trust Him. No matter how difficult the circumstance that I find myself in, I will trust that the Author of my life is helping me to write my story. Because my story is His story as well. In that truth will I find my purpose.

I won't let the fear of failure stop me from moving towards my purpose. I understand that making mistakes is actually part of the cycle of learning. Mistakes can make me stronger and wiser if I adopt the right mindset.

Because of this, I can get off the road of regret and self-condemnation. Each day gives me the opportunity to begin anew. The choice is mine to take a different path. And, so, I choose to let go of fear. I choose to let go of resentments. I choose to forgive myself. I choose to live wholeheartedly and love wholeheartedly.

*Lie #3: To live a meaningful life, I must do something 'big' by worldly standards*

Looking back now, the years when I was raising my children were probably the times when I most doubted my effectiveness. I was trying to build a career and be the best wife and mother I could be. Life was a juggling act of spinning plates and I feared that any or all of the plates could instantly come tumbling down.

The truth? There is a season for everything in our lives. And for each season, God has a plan and a purpose. My job is to discover and fulfill God's plan for my life as my life unfolds.

I look back now and see that every season in my life was precious and beautiful. Every season was a chapter in the story of my life. It wasn't always fun or easy, but every season was beautiful. And every season was significant in shaping me into the person I am today.

The truth is that, with all the highs and the lows of life, the joys and the pains, I was exactly where I needed to be. God's plan for my life was working in my life. God's plan was being accomplished through every load of laundry I did, every dinner I cooked, every diaper I changed, every nursery rhyme I sang, every prayer I said, every booboo I kissed, every school project I supervised, every piece of advice I gave, every joke we shared, every time I fell short as a mother and a wife and asked God for forgiveness… I was living out God's plan for my life, I was writing my story and leaving my legacy.

My job is to be my authentic self so that I can fulfill my divine purpose faithfully, season by season. My job is to show up and be present in life. My job is not to act as someone who has no goals but rather with intentionality I will pursue God's plan for my life. Recognizing that life is fragile, my resolve is not to take my life or my loved ones for granted. With intentionality I will live with more conviction, and love with more depth.

Whether or not there is a crowd applauding, I will keep showing up to life, and I will keep pursuing my God given goals.

That I pleased Him, is enough for me.

So, I continue to march onwards, with that knowledge. I press on, knowing that I am not doing it in my own strength, but with God's strength. I press on, in moments big and small. Nothing I do is insignificant. I will finish what I was put on this earth to accomplish.

I will leave my mark, to the glory of His name. I will be true to what God has called me to do. God's specific plan for my life is the only benchmark against which I will chart my success!

~~~~~~~~~~~~~~~~~~~~~~~~

"I wanna say I lived each day until I died
And know that I meant something in somebody's life
The hearts I have touched will be the proof that I leave
That I made a difference and this world will see

I was here: I lived, I loved
I was here: I did, I've done…

I just want them to know
that I gave my all, did my best
brought someone some happiness
left this world a little better
Just because I was here"

*From the song "I was Here" by Beyonce*
~~~~~~~~~~~~~~~~~~~~~~~~

**"...[What is secure in your life?] You are merely a vapor [like a puff of smoke or a wisp of steam from a cooking pot] that is visible for a little while and then vanishes [into thin air]." – James 4:14 AMP**

**"The great use of life is to spend it for something that will outlast it." – William James**

~~~~~~~~~~~~~~~~~~~~~~~~~~~~

I must have been about 8 years old. My mother was out and I was left in the care of an older cousin, Sister Bea. Bored, I wandered into my parent's room and decided to play *dress-up*. I tried on several pairs of my mother's high-heeled shoes
~~~~~~~~~~~~~~~~~~~~~~~~~~~~

before turning my attention to the impressive display of cosmetics on her dressing table. I liberally applied several shades of eye shadow and lipstick. With a satisfied grin, I turned my head from side to side, admiring myself in the vanity mirror.

But my makeover was not yet complete. I grabbed my mother's perfume and spritzed myself behind each earlobe, as I had watched her do. And then I closed my eyes, savoring the moment when the soft, floral fragrance delightfully wafted into my nostrils.

When Sister Bea eventually found me, she was beside herself. Not only had I made a mess in my parent's bedroom but, also, the scent of my mother's perfume still lingered powerfully in the room. How would she ever explain that I had been left unsupervised long enough to make this mess?

What struck me about that moment, though, was that rather than cleaning up the mess I had created, she frantically tried to air out the room first. Only when she felt that the fragrance had sufficiently faded, did Sister Bea turn her attention to the clean up.

How a small vapor-mist of perfume can diffuse and permeate a large room with its beautiful fragrance is a phenomenon that still fascinates me to this day. The mist itself is visible for just a few seconds, however the aroma lingers for a long time. Isn't that the same way one person can impact the world powerfully, for generations to come?

*"What is secure in your life?"* – James 4:14 AMP

This phrase jumped out at me and so I looked up the meaning of the word 'secure'. *It means to be "fixed, so as not to give way, or be lost".*

And, so, this is the meaning I get from James 4:14: *"Aba, like a vapor-mist your life on earth is brief compared to eternity, but your "fragrance" is what you will leave behind. What fragrance will you leave, Aba?"*

Our *fragrance* is made up of the beliefs and the behaviors that are fixed, consistent and secure in our lives; the things we repeatedly do.

Our *fragrance* is the legacy we leave behind after we are gone.

What is secure in your life? What do you believe in? What do you stand for? What principles define how you live your life? What do you consistently do? That will be your legacy and that is what you will be remembered by.

Often the world experiences the sweet aroma of just one major action or event in a person's life. And that one event represents their legacy. But the truth is that it would have taken years of intentional behavior to get the person to that big moment in their lives.

American civil rights activist Rosa Parks' act of defiance in refusing to relinquish her bus seat to a white passenger, and the ensuing Montgomery Bus Boycott is what the world largely knows about her. What is lesser known is that at least 12 years before that defining moment in civil rights history, and for decades afterwards, Rosa Parks was a civil rights activist. That is who she was, that is what she stood for, and that was the legacy she left behind.

When I worked as a pharmaceutical sales rep in Hartford, Connecticut, our team's main business strategy was borne out of the 80-20 rule. That is to say, the bulk of our selling efforts were focused on the 20% of our customers that brought in the most sales. We called those physicians our "top docs".

Dr. Kelvin was one of the top docs in my territory. He owned a large, thriving medical practice that employed several other physicians. Many of Dr. Kelvin's patients were the ideal candidates for my team's portfolio of depression, diabetes and heart failure medications and therefore his support for our products could make or break our business.

So my partners and I made sure that we were in Dr. Kelvin's office several times a week. We would support his office with samples of medication and patient literature. And, at least once a week, one of us on the team (often myself) would deliver breakfast or lunch to Dr. Kelvin's office. I prided myself on having built a solid working relationship with Dr. Kelvin and his staff.

Dr. Kelvin himself seemed largely unaware of the rock star status we pharmaceutical reps accredited to him. He was a kind, humble, Christ-like, soft-spoken gentleman. He was active in his church and regularly served on medical mission trips. He was a compassionate physician who truly cared about his patients.

Occasionally, we brought expert specialist physicians into Dr. Kelvin's office for lunch-and-learn sessions on various medical disorders. But whether it was our regular weekly lunch meeting or a special event, I noticed that there was one thing that Dr. Kelvin always did; he bowed his head and said a short prayer before every meal.

It's been a decade and a half since I left that sales position in Connecticut, but my memory of Dr. Kelvin's expression of faith – his simple act of bowing his head to pray before every meal – once a week for five years, is the powerful lingering aroma that he left with me.

What I have realized is that a powerful legacy may not necessarily be the result of a huge event witnessed by thousands of people. A powerful legacy can be borne out of a thousand consistent, everyday actions that are the result of what you stand for.

My promise to myself, henceforth, is to live my life with intentionality. I want my actions to reflect what I stand for. I want my time on this earth to mean something. I want my life to count. I want to leave an aroma that lingers after my time on earth is done.

So, from now on, I will no longer seek to just have a 'nice' day. Instead, I will have a day that is intentional, kind and true to what I stand for. I will live each day purposefully and joyfully. I will spread hope today. This is my life, and this will be my legacy. This is my life, and it will be fragrant.

**“Each time you say, 'I love you,' you are really saying 'I am here for you.'” – Robert Holden**

**“Love…transcends…time and space.” – Amelia Brand from the film Interstellar**

**“I close my eyes and I'm seeing you everywhere**
**I step outside, it's like I'm breathing you in the air**
**I can feel you're there”**
**(From “Fall on Me”, sung by Andrea Bocelli)**

~~~~~~~~~~~~~~~~~~~~~~~~

“Love you and leave you not,” was how my mother would sign off from our phone conversations.

I am a firm believer that we can never say “I love you” often enough to our loved ones. Also, I believe that it's important
~~~~~~~~~~~~~~~~~~~~~~~~

to always say a loving goodbye before taking leave of a loved one. Life is fragile and the truth is that tomorrow is not promised to any of us.

It's not that I have a fatalistic attitude towards life; it's just that I have experienced the pain of not getting to say goodbye to a loved one.

It happened on February 2, 2005. I was told that my mother had had a regular day. They said that she had been in a joyful mood that day. She had gotten her eyebrows waxed and then spent the rest of the day at Little Flower Montessori School, the school she had founded almost twenty years earlier.

My mother's career as an educator had spanned almost 40 years; many of those, years in which she had taught kindergarten. In her last few years, she had been semi-retired; however on that fateful day, she had spent several hours at her school. They say she visited each classroom and then lingered in the kindergarten class; calling those children "my heart".

In the evening, she watched the news and then chit-chatted with my father as they shared a mango. Just before 10pm, she discussed her plans for the following day with my brother – she had a busy day scheduled. After that conversation she went upstairs to bed. Thirty minutes later she had passed away.

With no warning, my beloved mother was gone from this world; gone much too soon from me, leaving me heartbroken and stunned, struggling to make sense of it.

As an adult, I had always lived in a different country than my mother. The technology of the early 2000's offered much more limited options for communication than present day and we had to make do with expensive international calling cards. So my phone calls to her were mostly limited to the weekends.

I looked forward to our weekend chats. However, that last weekend of her life, I didn't call her; instead I called my friend. Realizing that I did not have enough units on my calling card to make two phone calls, I made the decision to instead call a friend who was going through a difficult time. I made that decision after having this distinct thought: "Call your friend. Mummy will ALWAYS be around. Tomorrow you can go out and buy another phone card." But I forgot to buy a new phone card the next day, and the day after that. Three days later, Mummy was gone…

My relationship with my mother evolved through different phases as I grew up. The many photos of tender moments between my mother and me as a baby and the anecdotes of precocious and hilarious things I did and said to her as a young child bear testament to the warm, loving relationship that existed between my mother and me as a young child.

However, as I got older, I felt that my mother was too hard on me. I spent a lot of my childhood feeling intimidated by her. I was told that, as her firstborn, she wanted to raise me right so that I could also set a good example for my younger siblings, but that was cold comfort for a little girl who felt like she was buckling under the weight of her mother's critical eye and sky-high expectations. I often felt that my life was regimented and restricted, not privileged and exciting, like people thought.

By my early teen years, I had become distant, moody, withdrawn, finding my solace between the pages of the books that I voraciously devoured. I remember, at age 14, looking up to the sky and asking God why He had given me the most impossible mother ever.

But when I was 15, something miraculous happened. I came home from school one day and recounted a funny incident that occurred in one of my classes. My mother listened intently and then burst out in the heartiest laughter I had ever heard from her.

After that day, we began to have more of those mother-daughter moments. I remember at 15 thinking that perhaps my mother wasn't as bad as I had thought – especially if I kept up with my chores. At 16, I remember looking at her one day and noticing how absolutely beautiful she was. At 18, she and I had a falling out because she categorically disapproved of my boyfriend. But when he broke my heart, it was to no other place but her outstretched arms that I ran.

At 20, it dawned on me that my mother was the best friend that I had. She was also my fiercest ally, my prayer warrior and my confidante. And that is what she was to me till the day God called her home.

Raw with grief, I mourned the light that had been extinguished from my life and I contemplated the many things I could have said that would now forever be unsaid to my mother. I never got to tell her about how my week went. I never got to tell her that, now that I was a parent myself, I understood the enormous weight of responsibility that a parent carries in shaping their child's life, and that I finally 'got' her. And although I tried to show it in a bunch of different ways, I don't think I ever seized the opportunity, directly and eloquently enough, to tell my mother just what debt of gratitude and love I owed to her.

The intense pain of missing out on the chance to say that final goodbye to my mother lingered for a while. But one morning, with the slow dawning of sunrise, memories of a thousand small, big, magnificent, ordinary, hilarious, frustrating, inspiring, disagreeable, loving mother-daughter moments and "Love-you-and-leave-you-not" goodbyes began to flood my soul. Each memory was a priceless reminder to me that we had loved each other deeply and fiercely and I felt an incredible healing balm to my soul.

In a world of a million goodbyes, we are not guaranteed the privilege of a final, meaningful goodbye moment with our loved one. But what we will have is a treasure trove of precious memories to draw on. And while we still have life, we have the ability to build even more beautiful memories.

Don't let an "I love you" go unsaid in your life.

And make every goodbye count.

# Mrs. Cato's Starfish

*One day a man was walking along the beach when he noticed a boy picking something up and gently throwing it into the ocean. Approaching the boy, he asked, "What are you doing?"*

*The youth replied, "Throwing starfish back into the ocean. The surf is up and the tide is going out. If I don't throw them back, they'll die."*

*"Son," the man said, "don't you realize there are miles and miles of beach and hundreds of starfish? You can't make a difference!"*

*After listening politely, the boy bent down, picked up another starfish, and threw it back into the surf. Then, smiling at the man, he said..." I made a difference for that one." – "The Starfish Story", by Loren Eisley*

**"I believe that every single one of us is here on this earth for a reason. I believe it's our life's work to figure out who we are, what we think, what our gifts are, and how we can make a difference in this world." – Maria Shriver**

***If I can stop one heart from breaking,***
***I shall not live in vain;***
***If I can ease one life the aching,***
***Or cool one pain, ...***
***I shall not live in vain.***
***"If I Can Stop One Heart From Breaking" by Emily Dickinson***

~~~~~~~~~~~~~~~~~~~~~~~~~~~~

My mother Mrs. Cato simply loved children. She always said that if she had had her way, she would have had ten children.

God blessed her with three biological children and in a teaching career that spanned almost four decades, she taught, influenced and loved scores more children.

But my mother's heart for nurturing children went beyond even that. When my siblings and I went off to boarding schools for our high school and university years, Mummy brought in younger children to live in our home.
~~~~~~~~~~~~~~~~~~~~~~~~~~~~

Typically, these children were from backgrounds that were less privileged than we had been blessed with. Usually it would be one child at a time; sometimes two. These children lived in our home for varying amounts of time. They were also given the opportunity to attend Little Flower Montessori School, the school my mother had founded.

My siblings and I would come home on school holidays to meet a new child living in our home. Initially we grumbled about it, because more children in the house increased the chores and the responsibilities on us. But, after a while, we stopped questioning my mother and just went with her flow (not that we had a choice!). And we lovingly accepted these children as part of our family. It wasn't hard to do, though, because each and every child was so lovable.

Back then, I had assumed that Mummy was just trying to re-fill her empty nest. It didn't occur to me then that my mother may have had another motive beyond keeping her home filled with the laughter of children. There was absolutely no material gain in this for her. In hindsight, I realized that Mummy had identified something special in each child that she wanted nurture. That was her main motive.

More than three decades later, the names and faces of some of these children have faded from my memory. But a few months ago, I received a Facebook message from Abena B. It took a few questions for me to recall who she was. Abena had lived in our home for about a year when she was nine years old. Fond memories of Abena came flooding back as I remembered the bright-eyed, intelligent confident little girl who had loved to read and loved school.

Excerpts of her letter read:

“Hi Sis Aba, I'm Abena B. I lived with your family between 1991 and 1992. I wanted to thank you all so much for your role in my life. I heard about Mummy passing away some years back… I'm a mother of a teenage son and I've been a registered nurse for over 13yrs. I'm now doing a specialty course in Critical Care Nursing. Thanks to Mummy for giving me a great start in life. I owe much to your family for a great beginning…”

I was so touched by Abena B's letter. To hear about the impact my mother had on a person's life, almost 15 years after her death, was truly a gift to me. After my conversation with Abena B, I felt a new dose of inspiration wash over me. I renewed my commitment to myself to live my life so as to make a positive difference in the world. As I did, I reminded myself of these three facts:

It doesn't take a grand gesture. But it counts.

It doesn't matter if no-one ever hears about what you did. It still counts.

It doesn't matter that the world may not think that what you are doing is important. Know that, to that one person, you made a world of difference.

Mrs. Cato was more than a kindergarten teacher. Over the course of her life, starfish by starfish, Mrs. Cato was a Destiny-Shaper and a World-Changer.

~~~~~~~~~~~~~~~~~~~~~~~~~~

***"...I've noticed something about people who make a difference in the world: They hold the unshakable conviction that individuals are extremely important, that every life matters. They get excited over one smile. They are willing to feed one stomach, educate one mind, and treat one wound. They... are satisfied with small changes. Over time, though, the small changes add up. Sometimes they even transform...the World." – Beth Clark***
~~~~~~~~~~~~~~~~~~~~~~~~~~

**"The end of a thing is better than its beginning…" – Ecclesiastes 7:8 NKJV**

**"There is no knowledge hard to acquire as the knowledge of how to live this life well and naturally." – Montagne**

**"God gave us the gift of life; it is up to us to give ourselves the gift of living well." – Voltaire**

~~~~~~~~~~~~~~~~~~~~~~~~~~~

"It doesn't matter how you start out in life, what matters is how you finish." These are words that my father reinforced to us as we were growing up.

His statement is one I have thought about many times throughout my life. There are incredibly talented people who
~~~~~~~~~~~~~~~~~~~~~~~~~~~

came out of the gate running. Early in their lives, they made great accomplishments in their fields of endeavor; created amazing opportunities for themselves and their communities and earned more money than they would be able to spend in a lifetime. Yet, despite their financial wealth, privilege, influence and glory – all the commonly used markers of success – they led sad, lonely, regret-filled and sometimes tragic lives.

I celebrated my 50th birthday recently. Reaching this milestone made me particularly reflective about my father's statement. At age fifty, I am aware that I likely have more years behind me than in front of me. I see my end in sight. This is not AT ALL a morbid thought, nor is it meant to be depressing. On the contrary, knowing that my days on earth are finite gives me the sense of urgency and excitement to strive to be my best self and to live my best life. And for the areas of my life where I haven't been doing that, to course correct.

So, I inevitably thought about my dear father, who is 81 years young. He is simply an amazing human being. He inspires me because he is someone who continues to live his life well every single day. When I look at him, I see a man who everyday gave his best to his loved ones and to his life's work. And I see a man who achieved greatness without losing his sense of self. How does a person do that? Is there a formula to his approach to life that I could discover and bottle?

My father, Ambassador Annan Cato, is in my opinion one of the most dedicated and respected career diplomats to have served Ghana. During the span of his illustrious 45-year career, my dad served on numerous postings, including the Ghana Embassy to Ethiopia, the Ghana Embassy to Italy, Ghana's Mission to the United Nations in New York, Ghana's High Commissioner to Canada and Ghana's High Commissioner to the United Kingdom and Ireland.

His work with the United Nations in the 70s and 80s was with the Human Rights Commission, where he was privileged to be the chairman-raconteur of the Adhoc Working Group of Experts on Southern Africa, a committee that was formed to document specific cases of human rights violations as a result of apartheid.

Back home in Ghana, my father also served in several government appointments, including Director of State Protocol, Chief Director of the Ministry of Foreign Affairs, and Secretary to the Cabinet of President John Agyekum Kufuor.

The life of a diplomat can be glamorous. And those glamorous experiences spill over to the children of the diplomat. I was born in Rome, Italy and experienced stints living in Ghana as well as in all the cities my father was posted to. As the child of an Ambassador, I got to live in Ambassador's Residences – beautifully furnished mansions equipped for entertaining and staffed with a personal cook, butler and chauffeur.

My dad was blessed to have personal staff who also doted on his family. And so, I have many fond memories. In Switzerland, Mr. Ahmed, the consummate professional chauffeur who drove me to school (fortuitously at a time when I was being bullied at school) would insist on opening the car door to let me out. I gladly let him do it, although I don't think my dad ever knew that he did that. In Canada, Mr. Maxwell the butler (who doubled as my ludo playing buddy) didn't hesitate to serve my friends snacks on a sterling silver tray, with all the butler panache he could muster. Mr. Hema, the butler in London, would have brought me breakfast in bed if I had requested it. I never did, though, only because if Daddy found out...

Throughout my childhood, it was the norm to watch my parents attend functions with dignitaries, world leaders, senior government officials and members of the diplomatic corps.

Our lives were very different than the childhood my father had experienced…

My father (whose name 'Annan' means 'four' in Fante) was the fourth son born into a large extended family. His father, James Samore Cato, was a manager of a transnational company, the United Africa Company, now known as

Unilever; while his mother Elizabeth was a baker. Tragedy struck the family when, at the age of thirty-three, Elizabeth died giving birth to twins. Both babies died as well. My dad told us that one of the few memories he has of his mother was seeing her lifeless body, the twins lying on either side of her. He was just six years old.

After his mother's death, my father was uprooted from the life he had known. He was raised by a *parental tribe*, which consisted of his father, Grandpa Samore, his father's sister, Aunt Emma and his father's brother and his wife, my Grandpa and my Grandma Cato, with whom he lived for much of his childhood. He said he had a happy childhood and was raised with responsibilities and expectations. I would imagine, though, that he had to work a little harder than the average child so he didn't fall through the cracks.

My father's success in life did not come easily; therefore he never took life for granted. It was important to him that we, too, stayed grounded. He did not want the glamour of diplomatic life to give his children a false sense of self. In fact, I think he was terrified that we would grow up entitled because of the lifestyle that we experienced as children.

So, he reminded us periodically that many of the perks we were enjoying were only as a consequence of his job assignment; and that those things didn't constitute our "real" lives. He would remind us that the day would come when he would retire from diplomatic life to a much quieter and simpler private life. He always concluded his talks by telling us that the biggest legacy he was leaving us was our faith, our education and his good name. The rest would be up to us to live our lives well.

My father is retired now, and continues to lead a full life, enjoying the rich relationships he has cultivated with his family and friends. He still maintains a busy schedule as husband to Grandma G, *Ebusuapanyin* (Family Head), and as Grandpa extraordinaire. He continues to work on special projects at the behest of his government, and whenever the opportunity arises, to pass on his knowledge and experience to the next generation of foreign service officers. He works on these projects with the same zeal and commitment that he showed for 45 years. He is a public servant in the truest sense of the word.

How did this remarkable man navigate his remarkable life? That's what I wanted to find out. So, one day, I called him up and, with no notice at all, I posed this question to him: "Daddy, who are you, and what is your philosophy about life?" Below are excerpts from his verbatim response.

*Well, I will say, I'm a simple guy who seeks to have a family, to do the best that I can in the profession that I selected and to do to others what I want them to do to me.*

*I detest injustice. I believe that every human being has value and should be treated with dignity and respect. When these are denied, I get deeply offended.*

*I'm at peace with myself. I take life as it comes.*

*I have had ambition in my life, but I'm proud to say that I did not take short cuts.*

*My aim was to enjoy what I was doing, do the best that I could, hope that I would have a comfortable life and also be as helpful as I could to those who would need my help in whatever way it was possible...*

*If you'd asked me, fifty-five years ago when my career started, no my ambition didn't go that far. Yes, I worked hard, and I hoped to become an ambassador one day. But along the path many other opportunities came my way and, when they did, I seized on those opportunities...*

*I don't think that I'm endowed with extraordinary attributes...However, hard work doesn't kill and I think I threw everything I had into what I had to do. That's who I am.*

*So, how do I summarize it? I am a simple guy who, in his lifetime, has achieved far more than he expected to achieve, and is very grateful for those achievements; but also someone who loves life, loves friendships, values respect and dignity that people are entitled to as their right, and is indignant where injustices are inflicted on people. That's my philosophy in life. I went through over 40 years with an impeccable work record. If you go to the Ministry of Foreign Affairs, there is nobody who will say that I took shortcuts. And, in the process, I think that I've earned some respect, which makes me extremely happy but also the more humbled by the recognition that has been given to me. Truly. I have punched higher than my ability, but at every stage I was accountable.*

*I have had my share of disappointments, but everybody goes through life with some disappointments. Pain? Sure, sure; there have been a few deaths: (my cousin) Nana's death and (my first wife) Rita's death… those were serious setbacks for me...*

*Losing my mother so young could have had a more serious impact. I would have loved that if my mother had lived, at some point in life, she would also stand there and look at me and say "aah, there's my son", and I would hold my mother's hand and say "this is my mother", that kind of thing. But that was denied me...So what I didn't have as a child, I gave to my children, whom I love very much and who are also my friends. My children's teasing… I would also have loved to tease my mother. And perhaps there's also a lot more about myself that I could have found out about from my mother: stories, anecdotes. So, with my children… I share these stories with you guys…*

*But life has been good to me. I have been blessed… So, that's where I stand.*

~~~~~~~~~~~~~~~~~~~~~~~~~~
~~~~~~~~~~~~~~~~~~~~~~~~~~

What did I learn from that conversation? Here are the nuggets of wisdom I gleaned from my father's life and legacy.

1. He has a clear sense of who he is – husband, father, public servant.
2. He discovered his mission – service to God and country.
3. He was clear about his philosophy of life – upholding the dignity and value of human beings; fighting against injustice; loving his family; maintaining cherished friendships; accepting life with its ups and downs; adhering to a solid work ethic; upholding the virtues of commitment, loyalty, gratitude and humility.
4. He never set out to build a reputation; rather, he set his behavior to be consistent with his philosophy of life. Therefore, what he built and has maintained throughout his life, is CHARACTER.
5. He found a career that he was passionate about and that was congruent with his personal philosophy and mission in life. Therefore, he viewed his career as a calling; not just a job. He operated in the arena of his strengths.
6. He worked harder than anyone I know. He never took shortcuts. He attributes his success primarily to his work ethic.
7. He seized opportunities that came his way.

8. He is a man of excellent habits. For example, throughout my life, his regular morning routine would be: wake up at 6am, spend about 20 minutes exercising, catch up on the news, take a shower, have breakfast promptly at 7am. And head out to work straight after breakfast. Now that he is retired, his routine hasn't changed much, except he goes walking for 45 mins to an hour, daily.
9. He possesses an extraordinary level of emotional intelligence.
10. I believe that the foundation of this was birthed out of his philosophy that all human beings are deserving of dignity and respect. And, so, whether he was interacting with a dignitary or not, my father has always treated everyone with the same level of courtesy and respect. This philosophy has allowed him to maintain enriching personal and professional relationships throughout his life. The respect he shows to others is a major reason why he is respected and loved by so many people.
11. He has never been entitled about life. He accepts that life comes with its ups and downs. He acknowledges that some things that he went through hit him really hard. Yet he continues to love his life. And life has loved him back.
12. He is a grateful person.
13. He stays humble.

# Custodian

**"A good name [earned by honorable behavior, godly wisdom, moral courage, and personal integrity] is more desirable than great riches…" – Proverbs 22:1 AMP**

**"A good person leaves an inheritance for their children's children..." – Proverbs 13:22 NIV**

**"Every generation must recognize and embrace the task it is peculiarly designed by history and by providence to perform." - Chinua Achebe**

~~~~~~~~~~~~~~~~~~~~~~~~~

Growing up, my father always had a busy schedule and so when I moved away to college and even when I transitioned into independent life, Daddy's phone calls were typically a brief check-in to make sure that I was okay.
~~~~~~~~~~~~~~~~~~~~~~~~~

But now that Daddy has been fully retired for about a decade, I have noticed a reversal of our roles; I'm the one who now calls intending to have a brief check-in, while he is the one who will often extend the conversation, wanting to get updates on how each and every one of us is doing.

Actually, let me qualify that. I will still get the brief "check-in" conversation from Daddy if I call during times that break his unshakeable daily routine; for example, during his morning exercise. Or, right afterwards, when he catches up on world news. And I would wager that only an electricity power cut could make Daddy linger on the phone on weekdays between 7 and 8pm, when he watches his favorite TV programs.

Also, I still have not come up with a conversation juicy enough to entice Daddy to be late for his weekly Wednesday afternoon 'boys-boys' get-together, where they meet "under a tree" at a coded location. The "boys-boys" are a group of retirees with an average age of 79. Daddy supplies the 'unfermented' freshly tapped palm wine. (N.B. I drifted into such a deep, pleasant sleep one hot afternoon after gulping down a cold glass of his palm wine that had been in the fridge, that I now dispute its "unfermented" status).

But I digress. When you do get a hold of Daddy outside of those ring-fenced times, your intended ten-minute phone call can easily go on for an hour, during which he will ask to speak with everyone at home. I usually put him on speaker phone as he regales us with amusing anecdotes that always contain nuggets of wisdom as well as glimpses into his extraordinary life.

Recently, I called Daddy, intending for the phone call to be a brief check-in. But, as usual, he was in typical charming form. We chatted extensively about a number of topics. And then I asked him how he had managed to maintain his integrity and his reputation in a career that spanned five decades. In response, Daddy told me about a reprimand he had received from his father – my Grandpa – when he was about 10 years old and in elementary school.

As a boy, Daddy told me that he was a handful; he would often disobey his parents and go off after school to play soccer till the sun went down, rather than go home to do his assigned chores and his homework.

After a typical afternoon where Daddy had been truant, his father called for him. My Grandpa looked down at him and in a deep stern voice, he asked my father in Fanti, *"Herh, wo dzin nye dɛn?"* (Meaning, "What is your name?").

Daddy duly responded, "My name is Annan", to which my grandfather belted, "Annan is your individual name. 'Annan' refers just to you. Tell me: WHAT is your name?"

"Cato", my father meekly replied, "my name is Cato". To which Grandpa continued, "Yes, your name is Cato. I passed on the Cato name to you, and one day you will also pass the Cato name on to your children. It is a name with a good reputation. Make sure you don't devalue what you pass on to your children."

My father said he never forgot his father's words to him that day, because that was the moment he began to understand that, in the circle of life, he was a custodian, passing a baton from one generation to the next. A family name of good repute had been passed on to him, and he, in turn, had the responsibility to live his life so as to continue to build, and not tarnish, the legacy of the family name that he would pass on to his children.

A legacy is anything handed down from the past, as from an ancestor or predecessor and also from mentors, teachers and leaders. Our legacy is what we leave behind when we are gone.

Legacies are passed down in many different forms, including these: wealth, possessions, position, titles, knowledge, skills, talents, leadership, vision, stewardship, character, reputation, wisdom, discipline, a healthy lifestyle, financial prudence, an abiding faith. All of these forms of amazing legacies, though, can be tainted and passed down in ways that negatively impact the generations to come.

I picked up some important nuggets of wisdom from that conversation with my father:

1. It is important for me to discover and appreciate all the legacies that have been passed down to me.
2. I must remember that I too, am a custodian. It is my responsibility to build upon, and not taint, those legacies I received, so that I, in turn, can pass on an even greater legacy to my children.
3. It is also my responsibility as a custodian not to pass on a tainted legacy, just because that was how my forbears did it. When we know better, we should do better.

A big burden of responsibility lies on my shoulders. The consequences of my decisions – positive or negative - could last for generations to come. I must remember that it's not just about me.

I am a Custodian.

# And Who Is My Neighbor?

*One day an expert in religious law stood up to test Jesus by asking him this question: "Teacher, what should I do to inherit eternal life?"*

*Jesus replied, "What does the law of Moses say? How do you read it?"*

*The man answered, "'You must love the Lord your God with all your heart, all your soul, all your strength, and all your mind.' And, 'Love your neighbor as yourself.'"*

*"Right!"*

*Jesus told him. "Do this and you will live!"*

*The man wanted to justify his actions, so he asked Jesus, "And who is my neighbor?"*

*Jesus replied with a story: "A Jewish man was traveling from Jerusalem down to Jericho, and he was attacked by bandits. They stripped him of his clothes, beat him up, and left him half dead beside the road. By chance a priest came along. But when he saw the man lying there, he crossed to the other side of the road and passed him by. A Temple assistant walked over and looked at him lying there, but he also passed by on the other side. Then a despised Samaritan came along, and when he saw the man, he felt compassion for him. Going over to him, the Samaritan soothed his wounds with olive oil and wine and bandaged them. Then he put the man on his own donkey and took him to an inn, where he took care of him. The next day he handed the innkeeper two silver coins, telling him, 'Take care of this man. If his bill runs higher than this, I'll pay you the next time I'm here.'*

*"Now which of these three would you say was a neighbor to the man who was attacked by bandits?" Jesus asked.*

*The man replied, "The one who showed him mercy."*

*Then Jesus said, "Yes, now go and do the same."*

*–Luke 10:25 -37 NLT*

~~~~~~~~~~~~~~~~~~~~~~~~~
~~~~~~~~~~~~~~~~~~~~~~~~~

Our neighbor Simon lived at the end of our street. I met him one brisk autumn afternoon as he jogged around our neighborhood. The first thing I noticed about Simon was his size – he was a towering, muscular man. I was impressed with how powerfully he ran; beast mode activated, as beads of perspiration dripped down his face. Undoubtedly he was in peak physical condition.

Simon and my husband Eddie developed a camaraderie and, every so often, Simon would stop by our house for a chat. They always seemed to have things to talk about. I mostly observed and chipped in the occasional comment. As far as I could tell, Simon and I did not have much in common.

To be honest, I was also a little intimidated by Simon. I didn't quite know what to make of him. It was clear that he guarded his privacy intensely. I didn't know much more about him beyond knowing what he did for a living. In my opinion, he was a man of contrasts. To me, he acted like an alpha male, yet I could sense that a deep vulnerability lay just below the surface. And although Simon exuded a confidence that to me, sometimes seemed to border on arrogance, he was at the same time profoundly humble.

One day, I overheard three of our neighbors discussing a situation that occurred between Simon and another neighbor, which had resulted in a momentary, unprovoked display of frustration by Simon. I felt offended on behalf of that neighbor. I wondered what caused this behavior, and if things would be awkward in the neighborhood for Simon, moving forward…

Several months passed by before it occurred to me that we had not seen or heard from Simon in a long time. I tried to dismiss the thought; we all led busy lives, after all. Still, I wondered if Simon was deliberately avoiding us neighbors. That evening, I came across a quote by Joyce Meyer: "You never have enough information to judge someone." Immediately Simon came to my mind.

The very next morning, we heard the news that Simon had passed away overnight. Some of the neighbors had heard the police and ambulance sirens. We later found out that months earlier, Simon had been diagnosed with cancer. He had not told any of us neighbors about his illness. We were told that he fought valiantly till the end.

Ironically, I got to know more about Simon in death than I did when he was alive. I heard about the joys, the triumphs, the challenges and the pain that had interwoven to form the unique tapestry of who he was. Simon was a complicated man. He had overcome many obstacles and accomplished much in his lifetime. I felt a profound sense of loss knowing that I had missed the opportunity to get to know this remarkable human being.

It made me sad when I heard about a distressing situation Simon had been going through in the months preceding his death. I wondered if the stress from that situation had been a contributing factor to his embarrassing meltdown with the other neighbor.

It made me really sad to know that Simon and his family went through his difficult last days with very little support. They lived in a neighborhood, but perhaps they did not feel that they had neighbors they could reach out to.

In the decade since Simon passed away, I have gained a greater understanding of what it means to be a good neighbor.

I learned that my neighbor is not just a person who lives in my neighborhood. In this journey called life, my neighbor is the person that God puts in my path.

I learned that my neighbor is sometimes different than me – in gender, in color, in culture, in creed, in their interests, in their world view, in their faith, in how they love. Those differences make them no less my neighbor.

I learned that if I only show love and kindness to the people who are the same as me, then I will greatly limit what God wants to do through me.

I learned that being a good neighbor starts with being non-judgmental and compassionate.

I learned that being a good neighbor often requires me to go outside my comfort zone to reach out to people.

I learned that being a good neighbor reflects the character of God.

I learned that being a good neighbor allows me to be the hands of God.

I learned that being a good neighbor allows me to serve the higher purpose for which God has called me.

I learned that serving God's higher purpose for my life is what spurs me on to be a good neighbor, because being a good neighbor is often not convenient.

***"Everyone you meet is fighting a battle you know nothing about." – Wendy Mass***

## Running Out of Time

**"Yet God has made everything beautiful for its own time..." – Ecclesiastes 3:11**

"It is never too late or too soon. It is when it is supposed to be." - Mitch Albom, *The Timekeeper*

"Consult not your fears but your hopes and your dreams. Think not about your frustrations, but about your unfulfilled potential." - Pope John XXII

~~~~~~~~~~~~~~~~~~~~~~~~~~

*My sister-friend Phoebe is intelligent, gifted and hard working. I knew that it bothered her that she had a lot of unfulfilled dreams. Still, she pushed forward and pursued her goals with diligence and hope. Recently, her mentor of almost 30 years, a person she greatly loved and admired, died unexpectedly. A couple of months later, a still*
~~~~~~~~~~~~~~~~~~~~~~~~~~

***grieving Phoebe sent me a message describing that her life had come to a stand still, because she felt paralyzed with the fear that she was "running out of time".***

***What follows is my response.***

Phoebe,

So sorry to hear about Mr. D's death. You were truly blessed to have had someone in your life who mentored you about life and faith, and who looked out for you the way that Mr. D did. My deepest condolences.

Sis, this feeling that you are running out of time, as uncomfortable as it is, could turn out to be a positive thing. Don't allow the feeling to overwhelm you. Rather, let it spur you on to use your time strategically and purposefully.

I recall experiencing similar after my mother died. So many well-wishers shared the positive impact Mummy had on their lives. When I returned to work after her funeral, I noticed that I had begun to feel very dissatisfied about what I was doing with my life.

At that time, I had a great career. And for a season, it was the perfect job for me. But as time went on after the funeral, I became more and more aware that there were other skills and talents that God wanted to develop in me. That is what ultimately led me to pursue my calling.

So be grateful for this feeling, sis; not afraid. Allow yourself to explore what you are being drawn to. Discover the purpose for which God placed you on this earth. I agree wholeheartedly with your quote "your dreams should frighten you". The journey to a purposeful life WILL take us out of our comfort zone. But don't let fear stop you.

God will equip you with everything that you need. Allow yourself to be still, and you will receive direction about your next steps. I have found that when I am anxious, it blocks my ability to hear from God. Refocusing my attention back to Him calms my fears, strengthens me and enables me to hear from Him again.

I hold on to the belief that I am exactly where God wants me to be; or if not, that God is still able to bring me back into the centre of His will for my life. God is working out His purposes in you, sis. Keep seeking His will. Keep dreaming!

You are not too old to realize your dreams. But I agree, there is a sense of urgency. All of us, whatever age we are, need to realize that our time on this earth realm is short compared to eternity, and therefore we must use our time on earth wisely.

My personal interpretation of the Bible verse, "I will live and not die (Ps 118:7)" is this: "I will not die till the day that You, God, call me home. Till then, I will live out every day that You have appointed for me to live; to the fullest, trusting in You and accomplishing Your will for my life.

Don't just exist, sis; live every day to the fullest. Appreciate each moment. Your life may not have turned out as you thought it would, but life is still beautiful.

For a lot of years, I used to view life as a series of 'perfect' goals to be attained. No sooner had I achieved one goal (job, car, husband, child, house etc.) than I would set off to achieve the next, often without taking the time to enjoy the moment and be grateful for my blessings.

Now I appreciate that life is also about the journey. Now I appreciate the value of being present in every moment.

Now, even when the road is long, winding and difficult, I strive to stay present and to stay grateful, understanding that no experience in my life is wasted. Because now I understand that God uses everything we go through - the good, the bad, the ugly - to accomplish His will for our lives.

Trust Him. Be present. Live fully. Be grateful for your life's journey.

God will fulfill His purpose in your life.

Stay the course, sis.

Love always x

# *Family...*

# *Chicken Light Soup for an Effutu Soul*

**(Aba's Facebook post, February 2016)**

**"There is no one who does not like soup with fish in it." (Everyone desires good things.) – Igbo proverb**

~~~~~~~~~~~~~~~~~~~~~~~~~~

Yesterday I prepared a wonderful Light soup (using chicken and tasty mushrooms) for lunch. But when I got home in the late afternoon, I realized that Edmund Andah didn't eat any of it. I assumed it was because he had an evening dinner program. But, today, he dropped a bombshell on me! He told me that my Chicken Light soup (with tasty mushrooms!) "doesn't cut it" for him!!!

"Whaaaat?" I said, as blood rushed to my ears.

"Well, I like my Light soup to have a variety of meats..." he responded.
~~~~~~~~~~~~~~~~~~~~~~~~~~

"But WHO mixes chicken and meat in Light soup? We NEVER did that in my house growing up," I retorted defensively, my voice now an octave higher.

"Well, how about adding fish?" he sighed. "I mean, you don't have to do it if you don't want to. But I'm just telling you that chicken by itself in Light soup doesn't cut it for me."

We ended the conversation with me agreeing to add fish to my Chicken Light soup.

But this is what blew me away. I make this dish about once every 3 weeks. This means that in 20 years of marriage, I have cooked approximately 347 pots of Chicken Light soup (with tasty mushrooms!).

Why am I just hearing from hubby, after 347 times, that my Chicken Light soup (with tasty mushrooms!) "doesn't cut it" for him?!?

Moral of my story:

Pre-marital counseling should be expanded to include a thorough discussion of each person's Chicken Light soup preferences!!

**Eddie's Response:**

Ok. I think I need to mount a defense. As far as I'm concerned there are three, possibly four versions of soup. Light, palm-nut, groundnut and various amalgamated versions of these. Light soup, for me, is better the more inclusive it is. This view was further consolidated by a year living and working at Mampong Akwapim. I have tolerated more segregated versions of light soup in marriage out of an abundance of caution and the need for domestic harmony.

However, this last episode was, in my opinion, designed to just test my tolerance. In an effort to improve my health, a diet has been imposed on me, despite my loud protestations. I have quietly suffered a lot of indignities, including, I am ashamed to say, tofu bacon.

Dear friends, the quality of light soup depends on the juices that seep from the meats into the soup and gives you a mouthful of flavors that burst with vivid sensations and tickle those taste buds.

Said soup was, however, made with store-bought chicken and highly sanitized mushrooms. Chicken had probably never stepped outside of its narrow wired enclosure and had, thus, not been exposed to the elements and environment designed to add extraneous elements to its meat.

Mushrooms, I suspect, were grown in a lab. Nothing 'earthy' about it. *Dadaba*[4] mushrooms. But, on enquiry, I'm told the quantum of mushroom was increased in the soup in order to meet my daily requirement of vegetables! Can you believe this? Is it even a vegetable?

The soup did not have any particulate matter swimming in it, the hallmark of any good soup. It was impossible to take a spoonful of it without avoiding any mushrooms. Soup was too clinical. I would call it broth. The type you can get in a can. The soup you get when you have a fever.

I only suggested that light soup should be more inclusive. Be it chicken soup or, in this case, mushroom soup.

I'm even ashamed, as an Effutu[5] man, to admit to some of the girly things that are being forced down my unwilling throat.

Please if I have to have the so-called 'Chicken light soup', give me Chicken Light soup for an Effutu soul.

**Selected Comments from the Post:**

- What! And you never noticed? Did he eat your earlier creations? Just to please you?

[4]'Dadaba' is Ghanaian slang word for a "spoiled" or pampered child
[5]The Effutu area is located in the Central Region of Ghana

- And 347 chicken light soups later, you never picked up any signal that he wanted fish in the light soup? Hahahahahahaa!

- Chicken and fish light soup is delicious...use big fish...cut up of course!!! Lol

- I'm learning...Never been a chicken light soup person myself. Told my fiancé that I'm happy with 'United Nations'[6] light soup with dried fish and meat ensemble.

- Hmm looks like those American mushrooms don't work for the coastal Fanti man. Sooner or later he needs his fish...I guess the moral of this is we need to speak out (in love and a respectful way) about what we would like? Or is it to patiently wait and our day will come one fine day? Counselor, tell us!

- Chicken and fish? What a combination!! Marriage counseling should really be expanded. Lol

- Hilarious but packed with lessons to learn especially for 'beginners' like us.

[6]'United Nations' Light Soup, as the name would suggest, contains a variety of meats, fish and apparently chicken

- How!?! Add anything to chicken light soup and you've destroyed it. Aba, sorry okay?! Talk about compromise...

- I'm with you on this one. Chicken light soup should be nothing but chicken. You learn something new every day though. Very interesting.

- I'm with you ladies. Chicken light soup is just that. Light soup with a variety of meat and fish doesn't have chicken. Although I might be persuaded to use smoked chicken with a mixture. Thanks for the smiles this morning Aba.

- Thank you! Chicken light soup is exactly that. Not United Nations chicken light soup! But we learn something new every day. Tell us how your UN Chicken Light soup goes!

- Absolutely! Post marital counselling nonexistent. The things that we endure in the name of peace and compromise. Hmmmmmmm…

- I think this post is more important because couples are usually in a whole different world before their nuptials and so many things are overlooked which "suddenly" become issues after marriage.

- Aba Cato Andah, I add salted beef to my Light soup. It's very unhealthy but it cuts it for me. I'm with husband yours! Mushrooms (tasty or otherwise) don't cut it for me. It's a fungus!

- Aba, you've made my day. Body language lessons should be included in pre- and post-marriage counseling as well. This is too precious. Btw, while you're at it, go over the entire menu this time forward. I think we all need to take stock too before we're 'shocked'.

- I used to make my "famous" curry chicken two or three times a month... for YEARS... then one day Mike finally told me he never really cared for it. When I asked him why he never bothered to tell me, his answer was this... "Well honey, if you took the time to cook for me, I was going to eat it without complaining." Sweet answer…but man, I miss my curry chicken, lol!

- Give the man the Light soup that he wants, wai. Some of us prefer a forest soup, having all the beasts of the fields and birds of the air represented! We didn't live in your mother's house, wai! Lol...I still dey laugh. Edmund, let's insist on our rights to forest Light soup.

- I sometimes think I just started getting to know my husband after 10 years of marriage or so.

- Everyone changes as time passes by and we grow up.

- Inclusive light soup politicians, where are you? This is the manifesto to win hearts and stomachs with. Eddie, I feel your gustatory longings...

- Eiiish! Aba, in fact, I can see poor Edmund has been subjected to treatment not befitting an Effutu gentleman. Ebei! On top of that, the flavors he craves were picked up from the Mampong Akwapim mountain range and you of all people, Aba, should have that running through your veins. My sister, the case is settled. Be up and doing.

- In the matter of Mrs Aba Cato Andah (plaintiff) vs Owura Edmund Andah(defendant), it is the ruling of the court that henceforth the plaintiff shall cook light soup as specified and desired by the defendant.

- I must confess my chicken light soup is exactly as Aba does it without the fungus.

- Edmund Andah, I have a lawyer friend who specializes in soup litigation.

- Hahahahahaaaa Edmund I'm giving you a standing ovation right here!!!! Zoo soup all the way!

- My dear Aba, please sit down. It's okay to be a bit *sloooow* to connect the dots, but 347 times??!!?!!! Were there no signs? No clues?? Did he ever ask for seconds or left overs...??? Talk to me…

- It is a fungus, Aba, the man is drawing the line at double helpings of a fungus...can you blame him?

- Aba Cato Andah.... with this defence dierrrrr! PLEASE make the UN light soup...with chicken, goat, cow, sheep...what else?Oh, and fish!

- Just think that the number of days is almost equal to one full year of daily and continuously drinking soup under duress!

- Aba, I love it! So many lessons in this bowl of light soup! Cracking me up.

- Oh I am dying of laughter here Aba!...Men!

- Aba, great lesson but can't really stop laughing. Lolllll

- Aba, I was also raised not to mix chicken with other meats (or fish) in light soup. Haha. Let us know how your new recipe is received.

## The Good Doctor

**(Written on Doctor's Day, 2017)**

**"...Do all to the glory of God." – I Corinthians 10:31 NKJV**

**"… A life lived in service to others is worth living" – Albert Einstein**

~~~~~~~~~~~~~~~~~~~~~~~~~~~~~~

I think everyone should bring his or her spouse to work for a day. It's important because it gives you the opportunity to get to observe and appreciate what your spouse does.

I never quite fathomed the level of sacrifice and dedication that healthcare professionals put into their work, till I saw it firsthand.
~~~~~~~~~~~~~~~~~~~~~~~~~~~~~~

Since the day we got married, I had been asking my husband Eddie to let me watch him perform surgery. That dream finally came true when I had the privilege of watching Eddie bring my cousin's baby into the world.

Every birth is a beautiful and miraculous event and this birth was no different. A sweet atmosphere filled the operating theater as my niece made her entrance into the world.

But for me, the privilege of seeing my husband do what he does best, with such skill and command, was something I will never, ever forget. I had always known that Eddie is an amazing and devoted doctor. But nothing compared to the privilege of experiencing a working day in the life of the Good Doctor.

I SAW him wake up at 4.30am and review his patient charts.

And then I SAW him leave home to do his first surgery of the day at 7am.

My cousin's C-section was his 2nd surgery that day; then I SAW him go into another C-section shortly after that.

I SAW that he delivered 4 babies yesterday morning before even getting to the office.

I SAW that he had a full day of patients in the office before going back to the hospital at the end of day to check on his postoperative patients.

And, in that operating theater yesterday, I SAW the respect Eddie commands from the nurses and all the surgical staff. I SAW Eddie's amazing skill and compassion at work.

My heart burst with pride and the whole time I was in the operating room, tears were unabashedly running down my cheeks.

In my heightened emotional state, I giggled too loudly as the baby was being born, causing the surgical team (as well as the surgeon!) to look at me in surprise.

During the surgery, Eddie's phone rang and since no one was picking it up like they usually did, I took it upon myself to answer. I told the person to please call back later because he was busy at the moment. Turned out it was an emergency room doctor, and a few seconds later, when Eddie asked who had called, the nurse said "It was Dr. So-and-so, but it seems your wife hung up on him". Incredulously Eddie said "Aba, did you hang up on Dr. So-and-so??"

Needless to say, there is a strong possibility that Eddie may never again allow his wife into his operating room!!

Nevertheless, witnessing that day was a privilege I will never, ever forget. Eddie, I see you. I see your dedication; I see your passion; I see your toil.

I am *sooo* proud of you. And I've got a huge crush on you.

Thank you for doing life with me.

Your wife

# Son Shine

"You are my sunshine, my only sunshine… you'll never know dear, how much I love you…" – (From "You are my Sunshine", sung by Johnny Cash)

*Our son Archie wasn't planned. We had decided that we would not have children right away. We wanted to spend some years enjoying each other, building our careers and traveling. But then we got the best wedding present ever when a month after the wedding, we discovered that we had gotten pregnant. Did I mention that my husband was an OB/GYN resident at the time? Lol. Before I found out I was pregnant, I had a dream in which I was in a very dimly lit room. And then, a light began to glow in the center of room. I suddenly felt a feather-light tap on my forearms and then I felt something being placed in my outstretched arms. Although I couldn't see what it was, I remember thinking to myself that this was a "precious gift". And then the dim room began to glow with the most*

***beautiful light. I woke up wondering what that dream meant. Not long afterwards, I found out; our SonShine was coming into the world. Archie has been a light in our lives in every sense of the word. Brilliant and extraordinarily multitalented, Archie also has an incredible way with people which will take him very far.***

~~~~~~~~~~~~~~~~~~~~~~~~~~

My dear Archie,

My baby, my precious firstborn Son. I can hardly believe you are an adult now. You have grown into a young man we are all incredibly proud of!

On this occasion of your 21st birthday, here is some wisdom for you to keep in your heart.

Keep God first, Son. Learn fully what that means, and never take the precepts of the Lord lightly!

Let God lead you in all your endeavors, for then you will have good success in all realms.

Son, God has blessed you with amazing talents, some as yet undiscovered. May your gifts make room for you and bring you before great men and women. Remember, though, that there is no alternative to hard work and diligence. So never compromise your work ethic!
~~~~~~~~~~~~~~~~~~~~~~~~~~

Be You. As Auntie Susie said to you, be that highest, truest expression of yourself. Fulfill ALL your potential!

Stand out from the crowd. And stand up for what you believe in.

Be a leader, not a follower. Understand that servanthood is a key trait of every great leader.

Let integrity be your compass in all your utterances and all your dealings, Son. Your word must be your bond.

Treat others as you would want to be treated, Son.

Be mindful of your words. Choose to speak life.

Son, manage your Time, your Pride, your Anger and your Money and you will be unstoppable.

Travel. See the greatness of God from different locations and through different perspectives. It will make you a well-rounded individual.

Every human being is created in God's image. Remember, Son, that the light of God in you shines brightest when you allow yourself to also see God in the people you encounter.

So, treat every person you meet – whether prince or pauper – with respect and dignity. Regardless of their color, creed, age or worldview. No matter if their views are diametrically opposed to yours.

Son, be very careful of the friends you allow into your inner circle. Your best friends are a clear indicator of where you are also going in life. Iron sharpens iron. Don't forget that.

When someone offends you, forgive them. Forgiveness is one of the most amazing and powerful gifts you can give to yourself. Because forgiveness ultimately frees YOU.

Son, you are human, and you will make mistakes. Not that you should use your humanity as an excuse to misbehave. But when you do mess up, don't stay down. Rise up. Ask God and the person you hurt to forgive you.

Learn to always forgive yourself as well. Free yourself from regret, guilt or shame. Why? Because they are useless emotions that keep you stuck in life. Acknowledge your mistakes and missteps, gain new insights and choose to be better. And with that, move forward.

Son, the woman you love deserves nothing less than chivalry. Always treat her like a lady – with courtesy, kindness and consideration. Always!

Don't worry about the things you cannot change. Change the things you can. Seek God's wisdom so that you can know the difference.

Son, when life feels overwhelming, remember that you are never alone. You have a BIG God who is always by your side. He feels your pain, He heals your pain, and He fights your battles.

"There's no sadness Jesus can't feel
And there is no sorrow that He cannot heal
For all things work according to the Master's holy will
No matter what you're going through
Remember that God is only using You
For this battle is not yours, it's the Lord's"
(From *The Battle Is The Lord's,* by Yolanda Adams)

Happy 21st birthday, Son, I pray God's choicest blessings upon your life, today and always!

I charge you to impact your generation!

And please, eat your vegetables!

Love you fiercely, Mom

## *Alpha Mom*

**To Elissa; My Daughter, My Inspiration (Mother's Day, 2015)**

*A major turning point in my life came when I found out I was expecting a daughter. In that moment I felt a strong resolve to become my best self, so that I would be able to truly nurture, love and guide my daughter. Elissa's advent into the world was heralded by loud and indignant screaming, as she voiced her immediate and intense displeasure at being removed from the warm cocoon that been her home for 9 months. To this day, Elissa still knows what she wants. And she doesn't hesitate to voice it, or to go after it.*

*I knew I had to step up my game as a human being and as her mom, when she was three. I had been working with her on simple 3-letter words. Well, one day, someone asked*

***Elissa if she could read, and I said "No". And she replied, "Yes I can!" and then picked up another book and began to read a whole paragraph. Since that day I have continued to marvel at her intellect. I admire her work ethic and her leadership abilities. Elissa is compassionate and applies a spirit of excellence to every task she undertakes. Like her older brother, she makes us incredibly proud.***

~~~~~~~~~~~~~~~~~~~~~~~~

*Poem by Aba Andah (with the "cheesy" parts edited out by Archie Andah)*

ALPHA MOM:

"Alpha Mom", her card read.
Little does she know.
The tears,
My fears.
That I can't do it all,
I don't know it all.

"Alpha Mom", her card read.
She looks up to me!
She depends on me!
She believes in me!
~~~~~~~~~~~~~~~~~~~~~~~~

"Alpha Mom", her card read.
Little does she know,
How often I'm just winging it,
Sometimes faking it,
Praying I'm making it.

"My Inspiration" she calls me.
Little does she know,
That I am the one who basks in *her* glow.

I hope she knows – she beats in my chest.
I hope she knows – I gave her my best.
Even the times I was put to the test.

Alpha Mom? Not me.
Everyday new Grace,
Is what I crave,
To run this Race.

One day she will know.
The future will show.
But for today I will be her...
"Alpha Mom".

## *Priceless*

**(Christmas Day 2015)**

**Biribiara wɔ ne berɛ (Everything has its time) – Akan proverb**

~~~~~~~~~~~~~~~~~~~~~~~~~~

This Christmas, I was overwhelmed by the love from everyone in my family, but one gift simply blew me away.

The gift was inexpensive, yet priceless. It was the gift of encouragement from my son Archie.

Archie got me a book by Amy Poehler. I admit I haven't followed Amy closely, but it's hard not to notice how astronomically her career has taken off in recent years, both on TV as well as on the Big Screen.
~~~~~~~~~~~~~~~~~~~~~~~~~~

One thing Amy and I have in common is that we both have sons named "Archie".

This was my Archie's message to me:

"...Mom my gift to you is actually meant to be prophetic. I hope that, one day, Amy Poehler receives your book as a gift from her son Archie. I love you, and I believe in everything you were put on this earth to do..."

My tears flowed freely yesterday. And this morning I woke up early and put in a productive hour of work!

My child believes in me; what better motivation do I need to counter self-doubt and reach for my dreams?

From Archie's mouth to God's ears...

# *Cactus Dream*

**"Dreams are never concerned with trivia." – Sigmund Freud**

~~~~~~~~~~~~~~~~~~~~~~~~~~

My kids, when they were growing up, had different attitudes when it came to money. My son Archie has always been a strict saver. My daughter Elissa however, loved to shop, and there were a few times where I called her out on a purchase she had made impulsively.

One morning a few years ago, the following conversation ensued.

Elissa: Mom, I had a wild dream last night. I dreamt that I went to Target to buy a cactus. I had told you it would cost about 4 or 5 dollars. But after I bought the cactus, the salesperson told me I also needed to buy a "Cactus Starter
~~~~~~~~~~~~~~~~~~~~~~~~~~

Kit". When I asked how much it cost, they told me it was $709. I was surprised and asked what exactly was in the starter pack, to which she replied, "Uh, soil?" Then I said, "Mom's not gonna like this but oh well, I'll take it!" And I gave them your credit card. What does the dream mean?

Me: Why were you buying a cactus??

Elissa: I don't even know.

Me: Well, it might mean that perhaps your unconscious is telling you to thoughtfully consider whether you really need to buy something, as opposed to buying something just because you can.

Elissa (*shakes head and mutters under breath*): I knew I shouldn't have told my dream to a therapist!

**"Words are free. It's how you use them that may cost you." – KushandWizdom**

**"Like apples of gold in settings of silver is a word spoken in right circumstances." - Proverbs 25:11 NASB**

~~~~~~~~~~~~~~~~~~~~~~~~~~~

One day, several years ago, out of the blue, my family began to quote the things that they said I say the most.

I initially pretended not to listen, hoping that they would back off. But then curiosity got the better of me, so I asked them to list my twenty most used phrases.

Without missing a beat, they began to quote me. In no time, they came up with a list of twenty quotes.
~~~~~~~~~~~~~~~~~~~~~~~~~~~

Here is a sampling:

~~~~~~~~~~~~~~~~~~~~~~~~~~

"Archieeeee!!" (in a shrill voice)

"I KNOW you guys heard me calling you!"

"Go ahead!" (in response to which my kids have discovered that it's best to abort the intended action)

"Has anyone seen my glasses?" (a daily occurrence)

"My phone is dead!" (despite owning numerous chargers)

"I just want to look at the desert menu!" (after I've announced that I'm "so full")

"I over-ate."
"I'm going on a diet."
"I need to get back to the gym."

"Wake me up in 10 minutes, okay?" (never works!)

"I'm ONE person!"
"I'm not a robot!"

~~~~~~~~~~~~~~~~~~~~~~~~~~

It was hilarious, watching them go back and forth, imitating even my mannerisms and tone of voice.

But then I realized that something important was emerging from this simple exercise – I was able to stand back and see myself in a way I never had the opportunity to do before.

My most often used phrases were, in every sense of the word, a direct reflection of me! My humor, my wit, my quirks...

My quotes also reflected the areas of my life where I struggle, like maintaining a healthy diet and work-out regimen. And hearing my quotes was a great way to call me out for my displays of impatience and sarcasm!

I was also kind of disappointed. I like to think that I say lots of wise and encouraging things every day. Yet my "wise and encouraging" words didn't dominate their Top 20 list.

But then I realized that this was precisely the beauty of doing this exercise with my nearest and dearest!! Because, they are the people who know me best. They are the ones who see me in my unguarded moments. And, through them, I received an invaluable gift: the gift of self-insight.

It's a well-established principle in psychology that a person's thoughts directly influence their emotions and their actions. And the Word of God teaches this.

*"...for his mouth speaks from the overflow of his heart.." – Luke 6:45*

My top 20 list was clear evidence of this. My words were a product of my thoughts. And through my words I could identify my stressors as well as the behaviors that detract me from walking in the purpose that God has ordained for me.

So now, armed with this new insight, I was faced with a decision. Continue as is? Or begin a process of changing the behaviors that don't serve me well?

The ball was in my court…

**"A wise man changes his mind sometimes, but a fool never. To change your mind is the best evidence you have one." – Desmond Ford**

**"You never have enough information to place a judgment on anyone." – Joyce Meyers**

~~~~~~~~~~~~~~~~~~~~~~~~~~

If it is indeed possible to be giddy with excitement yet feel sick to the stomach with trepidation, that was my experience. It was my first day as a Lower Sixth former at Achimota Secondary School in Accra, Ghana.

Achimota had been my school of choice four years prior, upon passing my elementary school Common Entrance Exam. Both my father and my grandfather had attended
~~~~~~~~~~~~~~~~~~~~~~~~~~

Achimota, and I had been looking forward to carrying on the family tradition. However, after spending the summer in Geneva, Switzerland, where my father had recently been sent on posting, my parents changed their minds and decided, instead, that I would stay on in Geneva for school.

I felt gutted; I had been excited at the prospect of boarding school life and reuniting with my elementary school friends who had also been accepted at Achimota. But I resigned myself to my situation and settled into my new school in Geneva.

Four years later, when my family moved back to Ghana, the opportunity presented itself again and I didn't hesitate to apply to Achimota to attend the two-year Sixth Form.

I was beyond excited when I received my acceptance; but as the time got closer, I grew increasingly nervous. For one, I had skipped a grade so that I was now a year ahead of my elementary school classmates. Secondly, I hadn't seen my old school mates in over four years, and I wasn't even sure if they remembered me. I wanted to just seamlessly blend in.

The incoming Lower Sixth formers usually started about six weeks after the school year had begun for the rest of the student body. Their later start was due to the timing of the release of the West Africa-wide Form 5 "O" Level exam results and the subsequent placement of students in the sixth form schools.

I arrived at school in the early afternoon on move-in day. I had been assigned to the D-Dorm in Kingsley House. I slowly climbed the steps into the house; blinking for several seconds as my eyes made the adjustment from the glare of the outside sun to the dimmer inside lighting. Taking a deep breath, I entered the main landing, turned left and entered the D-dorm.

D-dorm was made up of two rectangular chambers, an outer chamber and an inner chamber. The younger girls slept in bunk beds in the outer chamber, which was longer than it was wide. The outer chamber opened up into the inner chamber, which was wider than it was long. The inner chamber housed the older girls. The Lower Sixth formers got to sleep in the corners of the inner chamber; in specially designed box beds big enough to store a trunk (which held our clothes) and a chop box (where we stored our non-perishable food).

I arrived in time to get an early-bird pick for a box bed and I strategically settled on a corner box-bed that was close to a bay window. I relished the opportunity to access morning sunlight, as well as the relative privacy of an unobtrusive corner. I pulled out my trunk and began to unpack...

The afternoon sun was fading. Siesta time was over, and the dorm was abuzz with chatter and laughter. The girls were getting ready to go to the dining hall for supper followed by prep (the evening homework period).

Because my classes had not started, I decided not to go to prep. I sat quietly on my bed, not quite knowing what else I could do. I pretended to read a book. In reality, I was silently observing the other girls.

The girls had changed from their regular school uniforms to "house dress". House dress for six formers was a brown and white checkered skirt with a short sleeved white shirt, tucked in. Clothing not in compliance with school uniform regulations was termed "non-school" and could result in disciplinary action.

***Sarah***

I spotted her as soon as she entered D-dorm; her eyes crinkling as she smiled. She burst into rich laughter as several people called out her name. The term for that was "giving her fans". "Sarah Johnston!" a bunch of girls squealed in delight. And with that, I got to know her name.

Sarah's bed was on the other side of the dorm, almost diagonally across the room from my bed. Because there were not enough box beds for all the Lower Six formers in D-dorm, she had settled for a regular bed. It didn't seem to bother her, though.

The other thing I noticed about Sarah, was that nothing she wore complied with school regulations. She was 100% "non-school"!

Skirts were supposed to be front-button midi-length gathered skirts, in brown and white checkered cotton fabric. Her skirt was barely knee length, had a zipper at the back, and gathered into a flare. The checks on the skirts were supposed to be 1/8-inch squares. Sarah's checks must have been at least a full inch.

Sarah was not wearing the prescribed front buttoned short-sleeved white blouse specified by the school, either. Her blouse had cap-sleeves with a V-neck in the front, and a deep "V" at the back, with two straps crossing over at the back. And her blouse was simply too short to be tucked in; instead it sat cheekily on top of her skirt, allowing the observer subtle glimpses of her midriff.

But that wasn't all. She was now trying to figure out what pair of shoes to wear for prep. School regulations specified black flat shoes or brown sandals. However, the options that Sarah was deciding between were 2-inch white sandals with a criss-cross design or a pair of black patent pointy-toed flats; both pairs very blatantly "non-school".

Sarah couldn't make up her mind. She tried on the white pair and then the black pair. She walked a few steps, glancing at her image in the mirror as she did so. Then she discarded the shoes she had on in favor of the previous pair of shoes she had just tried on.

She went back and forth, trying on those two pairs of shoes for what seemed like an eternity. All the while, I sat on my bed; pretending to read, but surreptitiously and incredulously stealing glances at her. After about ten minutes of watching her do this, I made my decision; I would have nothing to do with that girl because she seemed shallow!

I stuck to my decision for less than twenty-four hours. One conversation led to another, and before long Sarah and I were eating together, studying together and going to church together.

The thing about life is that it is best not to assume anything about someone. Instead, hear their story. There is always so much more to a person than the 'snapshot' moment you may have observed in their life. That's why it's best to not judge people.

What I came to discover about Sarah was that she was anything but shallow. She was a boarding school veteran, having been in boarding school since age six. And after eleven years of having to conform to strict boarding school regulations, it just so happened that I encountered Sarah on a day when she just wanted to express her individuality and personal style.

As we spent time together that school year, I learned so much more about Sarah. I found that she was kind, sensitive, had a uniquely creative mind and loved to laugh. And the more I learned about her, the more I grew to love her.

I also discovered that Sarah had some pretty hilarious quirks. For example, whenever our group of friends gathered to eat together – usually our staple boarding house meal of gari (dried cassava flakes) soaked in hot water, shito (pepper sauce) and tuna – Sarah often volunteered to say grace. And if my memory serves me right, her prayer would go on for at least ten minutes!

Sarah would pray for her family and her friends, for success in our A-Level exams, for us to get into our desired courses of study at university and on and on… and on. As she prayed, the rest of us would open our eyes to glare at her in disbelief. At some point she would pause in her prayer, seemingly about to conclude, but just as we started to breathe a sigh of relief thinking we could finally get to eat, she would bring up yet another prayer topic, to the dismay of our grumbling stomachs!

It has been thirty-four years and counting since Sarah came into my life. She is one of the funniest, kindest, most empathetic human beings I have ever had the privilege of knowing.

In Sarah, I found a friend who has seen me through my best as well as my worst days. She is infinitely patient with me and has never failed to be there for me. I hope I have been the same for her.

Sarah is my prayer partner and, I call her my Holy Spirit Assistant (HSA) because whenever I got impatient about waiting on God to answer to my prayers, I would run it by her and receive sage advice plus an admonition for us to pray about it some more. I also call her "Jonathan" sometimes, because she is to me as Jonathan was to David.

I shudder to think about how much I would have missed out, without Sarah in my life, if I had not reconsidered my initial rash decision!

(July 10, 2019)

**“Friends come and friends go, but a true friend sticks by you like family.” – Proverbs 18: 24 MSG**

**"Friends are relatives you make for yourself.” – Eustache Deschamps**

**“We are family, I got all my sisters with me” – Song by Sister Sledge**

~~~~~~~~~~~~~~~~~~~~~~~~~~

My son got married last Saturday!

Over the past week and a half, we had close to fifty family members and friends travel to Davenport, Florida to attend Archie & Sarah's wedding. For a solid week, our house was abuzz with an endless supply of food, love and laughter. And
~~~~~~~~~~~~~~~~~~~~~~~~~~

at the helm of affairs were my amazing sisters, who made sure everything ran smoothly.

In addition to my biological sister and my sisters-in-law, my sister-friends showed up for me in unbelievable ways. My sister-friends represent every phase and decade of my life, from my elementary school days to my awkward teen years, my college and post-grad years and through the different phases of my family and professional life.

Prior to last week, some of them hadn't even met. Yet they banded together like life-long friends and stepped up in unbelievable ways – serving, cooking, doing airport runs, making sure that everyone was comfortable, and treating my family with the love they would show their own families. And even my sister-friends who couldn't make it to Florida stayed close in spirit with prayerful messages and phone calls.

On the morning of the wedding, after my makeup was done, I suddenly became overwhelmed with emotion, so Sarah and Ama pulled me aside to pray. Ama held my hand and Sarah rubbed my back. They asked God to remind me that I was gaining a daughter, not losing a son. But, even as they prayed with me, I noticed that Sarah's teardrops were bigger than mine and Ama was wailing even more loudly than I. Then Ama told me off for messing up my makeup!

One thing I know for sure? Family is not just blood. Family is of the heart. I have been incredibly blessed to have my sisters.

Oh, and we danced to a whole lot of 80s music last week!

To my Sisters – Ekua, Grandma G, Auntie Nana, Auntie Esi, Auntie Rosalie, Gerie, Katie, Susie, Sante, Barbara, Maame, Kwartemaa, Nana Ofosua, Sarah, Ama, Esi, Naa Kai, Janewa, Awo, Jane, Didi, Vivian, Dzifa, Bunny, Karen, Daphne, Anthea, Edith. Thank you. You truly enrich my life.

# *Outed*

**"Truth will out." – William Shakespeare, *Merchant of Venice***

**"Truth is like oil. No matter how much water you pour on it, it will always float." – Yoruba proverb**

~~~~~~~~~~~~~~~~~~~~~~~~~~~~

Growing up Catholic and having attended Catholic schools, it is perhaps not surprising that one of the most exciting events of my childhood was meeting Pope John Paul II when he visited Ghana in 1980.

Two years earlier had been an interesting period in the Catholic Church's history, because there were three Popes in 1978. I was old enough to understand the sadness at the news of the death of Pope Paul VI, the joy upon the election of his successor Pope John Paul I and then the absolute shock that
~~~~~~~~~~~~~~~~~~~~~~~~~~~~

reverberated worldwide when Pope John Paul I suddenly died, just 33 days later.

So, when Pope John Paul II – the first non-Italian Pope in recent history - was elected Pope against this backdrop, it generated massive interest worldwide. Pope John Paul II carried a message of love, unity and forgiveness and was well loved.

In Ghana, we were honored that the Pope was coming to visit our country, and the air was fraught with excitement.

On the first day of his visit, the Pope's route took him past Flag Staff House, (now Jubilee House) the seat of the Presidency. I was in class 5 at Christ The King International School. Because our school was located close by, the whole school gathered at a prime location to catch a glimpse of the Pope as he drove by in his Pope-mobile, to our frenzied excitement.

A couple of days later, I actually got to meet the Pope, when he held an audience with a group of children. The night before, I could not sleep because I was so excited. I attended the event with my cousin Rebecca who was five years older than me, my little brother and my sister Ekua, who was a toddler at the time.

As the Pope worked his way through the crowd of children, I was awestruck. Pope John Paul II exuded gentleness, humility and compassion.

When the Pope got to me, he stretched out his arm and took my hand in his. His palms felt huge and incredibly soft. Wordlessly, the Pope then moved on to my cousin Rebecca who was standing right next to me, carrying Ekua on her hips. The Pope picked Ekua up briefly, and as he did, he spoke in heavily accented English, asking Rebecca, "You are mother?" And then as he looked more closely at them, he answered his own question: "No, you are sister!" And he blessed them and moved on.

Later that evening, some of my aunties, uncles and cousins came to our house. Rebecca and I were the center of attention, as we recounted our experience.

Obviously, Rebecca's story was more interesting than mine, because the Pope actually spoke to her!

But when one of my aunties in a side-bar conversation, asked me "So what did the Pope say to you?" I couldn't resist spicing up my story just a bit.

I quietly told her that the Pope said I was a "good girl". My aunt, not having any reason to doubt my account, then repeated what I had told her, to everyone's hearing.

And, of course, Rebecca jumped up and outed me.

I remember the split second of stunned silence in the room, followed by my utter embarrassment.

And that's how I learned the lesson that truth is always revealed.

It definitely took a while for me to live that story down, though.

Tough Stuff...

**The greatest glory in living lies not in never falling, but in rising every time we fall. – *Unknown***

***How did I make it all these years? How did I make it this far?***
***Through the valleys and over the hills...***
***It was God's grace (God's grace) [4x]***
***I made it this far, By the grace of God...***
**From the song "God's Grace" by Luther Barnes**

~~~~~~~~~~~~~~~~~~~~~~~~~~

*Stepping into the Dream*

We had been married for more than a decade and the future on our horizon loomed bright. We were both settled in great careers and were building our dream home.
~~~~~~~~~~~~~~~~~~~~~~~~~~

That Christmas, Eddie pulled out a beautifully wrapped box and surprised me with a breathtaking diamond bracelet. I had never in my life owned such a costly piece of jewelry. Eddie was making good on the promise he had made to me twenty years earlier, when he told me that one day he would "dress me in gold". *Well, diamonds are great too*, I contentedly thought to myself. I felt incredibly blessed and loved. After years of hard work, our dreams were finally coming into fruition.

***Blindsided***

The year had started out busy. As exciting as it all was, balancing work and family life was a challenge for me. I often fell asleep in an exhausted heap by 8pm. Eddie began to complain that we weren't spending quality time together.

As the spring and summer unfolded, I noticed a growing strain in our relationship. I attributed the stress to the planning involved in building a new house. Also, we had gone way over budget for this new home. But I was hopeful that once we had moved and were settled in the new place, things would go back to normal.

The return to normalcy that I had hoped for did not materialize. I couldn't ignore the fact that Eddie was getting home later in the evenings. And I also noticed that he had become protective over his cell phone. Questioning him did not yield satisfactory answers.

And so, one night, I quietly got out of bed and went round to Eddie's side. I unplugged his cell phone and slipped it into the pocket of my dressing gown. Then I tiptoed into our bathroom and locked the door behind me. After a few minutes of scrutinizing, I sat down dejectedly on the cold tile floor.

"How could he do this to me?" I cried to myself. I felt abandoned, humiliated and angry.

### *Unravelling*

I bombarded Eddie with questions, but I was still dissatisfied; so like a seasoned private investigator, I began to monitor his calls and messages. I scrutinized his receipts and the bank accounts. If I stumbled upon an expense I did not recognize, I would launch into a tearful, hateful tirade.

I was raw with pain and my reaction was to strike back at him verbally; wanting him to feel a fraction of the hurt I was experiencing. In the heat of those tirades, I was oblivious to everything but the urgent vitriol I was intent on spewing at him; sometimes not even aware that our young children were within earshot.

"We won't get anywhere with your angry attitude and with your stance of moral superiority", Eddie protested. But his words did not register. I was too busy blaming him to realize that the deep resentment I was holding against him was an equally powerful destructive force threatening our family unit.

With every resentful, unforgiving thought, I gave away a little more of my power. I wasn't sleeping well, and I could barely eat. Looking back now, I see that I was on the verge of a nervous breakdown.

We started going for marriage counseling, but our behavior patterns did not change. One day at therapy, Eddie announced that he was tired of all the conflict and that perhaps we needed to take a break. I flipped and told him that if he left, that would be it. It was an unproductive counseling session.

A few weeks later, one balmy August night, the kids and I got home late one evening. Eddie wasn't home yet, so I put the kids to bed and then went into our bedroom to settle down. As soon as I flipped on the light switch, I noticed the subtle differences in the room. And then I spotted the note on my nightstand. Eddie asked me to forgive him but said that he needed space to figure himself out and that he couldn't take the arguing anymore.

He was gone.

During that same time period, I had resigned from my job to go back to school full-time to train as a professional counselor. As it turned out, our marital problems intensified shortly after I left my job.

So now, not only was I was jobless but I felt husband-less and awfully sorry for myself.

***"For He will command His angels concerning you..." – Psalm 91:11***

God-sent 'angels' came to my rescue daily. There were too many incidents to mention. Most of these angels never knew about my situation, nor were they aware that their encouraging words or thoughtful acts of kindness gave me strength for that day.

Loved ones rallied around me as well. My Pastor called me every morning at 5am to pray.

My brother Kobby challenged me to "think strategically and behave mindfully" whenever we spoke. One day, after I recounted something I had done, he looked at me and quietly said "Aba, that is not how to win." That 'call-to-arms' in his simple cautionary phrase has, on many occasions since that day, spurred me on in times of challenge to reevaluate my actions and change lanes onto a winning course.

September saw me reluctantly settling into the reality of our separation. Our conflicts were fewer but probably only because we didn't have much direct communication. In the evenings, Eddie would come around to the house after work and be with the children till they went to bed. During those times, I would retreat to the bedroom. And when he bade goodnight and left, I would sob into my pillow.

One day, in a conversation with my sister Ekua where I recounted all the things that had gone wrong in my life, she suddenly burst out, "Stop right there. Aba, do you hear yourself? Do you hear the negativity? You are losing yourself! Aba, you've got to fight to get yourself back!"

Her statement jolted me like a surge of electricity. She was right, I couldn't recognize myself. I desperately wanted to get myself back, but I didn't know how.

As December rolled around, I felt bone tired of this situation. By this point, Eddie had leased an apartment on his own, further dimming the light of my hope for a restoration of our marriage. I felt drained, defeated and lonely. Impulsively I purchased plane tickets to spend Christmas with my sister and left the next day with the kids. Eddie found out I had taken the kids to Canada for Christmas from a note that I had left in the house for him. The drama that could have ensued was probably averted by the fact that he sensed that I was at a very low point.

Christmas in Ottawa was wonderful, courtesy of my sister and brother-in-law. The kids got to make snow angels and go sledding. I also got the chance to sleep, reflect and do a lot of praying. One morning on a prayer line I had joined, the Bible study was from Judges 4, which tells the account of how the Lord miraculously gave victory to the Israelites against the Canaanite army, which had boasted 900 iron chariots. The prayer leader declared that she felt led to tell someone on the prayer line "the chariots are falling". I felt strongly that the message was for me.

However, towards the end of December, I called my father in Ghana and told him that I wanted to get a divorce. And I instructed him, as per our Ghanaian custom, to inform my husband's family in Ghana about my intention.

My father, wise sage that he is, listened to my rant without comment. And then he said to me, "You know, it's Christmas; the season of goodwill. Why don't you just wait till after the New Year to deliver the news? In the meantime, be kind and decent to Eddie. After all, the worst is over." And so out of respect for my Daddy, I agreed. At this point, there was no need to keep fighting.

"The worst is over, the worst is over…" I repeated to myself over and over again. I noticed that, for the first time in a long time, I began to feel a hope rising. Somehow, I knew that I was going to be okay. I resolved to rebuild myself mentally, emotionally and spiritually.

*The Chariots Are Falling*

Strengthened by my New Year's resolutions, I immersed myself in my coursework. I was learning so much about human behavior that was of immense benefit to me. I also discovered that having schoolwork to focus on took my mind off my situation. My prayer life intensified, and I began to experience peace like never before. I also stopped the toxic arguing with Eddie. I felt like I was slowly healing.

We enjoyed a simple belated family Christmas centered on the children. A week or so later, when Eddie came over, I invited him to join us for dinner and was pleased that he accepted. A couple of days later, he ate dinner with us again. That evening, instead of going into my room, I hung out with him and the kids in our family room for the rest of the evening.

Eddie began spending more and more time with us at home and sometimes he even stayed overnight. This time, though, the visits were non-confrontational, stress-free and fun. It was slowly beginning to feel like we were a family again. But, like the threat of overcast clouds on an otherwise sunny day, it bothered me that he still had his rented apartment. It felt like he was hedging his bets. However, I decided to pray to God for wisdom, strength and discernment of His will. As I prayed, I felt peace and so I just continued to focus on the things I could control: my healing, being intentional in my behavior versus reacting to my fears, and maintaining a peaceful home environment for our children.

Valentine's Day rolled around and I had no plans. The doorbell rang. I wondered who that might be, since Eddie usually just came in through the garage. I opened the front door and there was my husband with red roses in his arms and a suitcase by his side.

***Lessons from The Tunnel***

Our loved ones rejoiced. They saw it as a miraculous, glorious comeback; a mighty testimony for a marriage that had been restored by God.

And all of that was true; however, as the weeks and months unfolded, I realized that the process of restoration and rebuilding had only just begun.

Our marriage would never be the same because we were not the same. Our marriage had died and now was being reborn. It was a new normal. Our lives were not a fairytale, but rather an imperfect union of two imperfect people who had come through by the grace of God.

I discovered that I had a lot of work to do on myself. I had to let go of my shame and embarrassment. I also had to let go of my fear and start to look at myself as God sees me, instead of identifying myself as the unloved and abandoned wife. I learned to own my story and see myself as the resilient woman that I was.

Forgiveness has been an ongoing journey. It started with the decision to forgive. One of my biggest victories in my journey of forgiveness was overcoming the beast called resentment. In time, I came to recognize the manifestation of resentment when a minor issue like an unwashed plate would derail my resolve and leave me feeling upset. Upon self-reflection, I realized that it wasn't the plate I was upset about. My upset was rooted in lingering resentment for what I had been through. In my fight against resentment, I decided to daily renew my commitment to forgive my husband. On days when I felt low, I had to remind myself of my commitment, several times in the day. I call this daily journey “Walking in Forgiveness”. Arriving at Forgiveness also came easier the more I became aware of all the mistakes that I myself had made in this journey. So, walking in forgiveness meant that I had to forgive myself as well.

I developed the habit of constant reading, learning, reflection and prayer. I set an intention to adopt Hope as my shield through this journey. I learned to stay in tune with my emotions so I could readily pick up on the 'junk-thoughts' that easily beset me with fear. And I learned that keeping my mind filled with positivity and the power of God's promises were my best help to fight the compulsive urge to check his phone.

I identified three reasons that fueled my compulsive need to check his phone:

1) because my trust had been shattered
2) I felt insecure that he loved me and
3) when I was feeling disconnected from him

I decided that until I could re-learn to trust my husband, I would trust the God who had brought him back to me. I continued to work on building my self-esteem and learning to truly love myself. And when I did feel disconnected from my husband, I learned to mindfully identify if there was an issue we needed to sort out, or if we needed to make time to connect with each other.

Here are some other lessons that I learned:

I'm 100% responsible for my actions at all times.

Nobody can make me act (or react) in a certain way.

Two wrongs can never make a right.

It's better to be loving, than to be right.

It's better to be understanding, than to be right.

It's better to be kind, than to be right.

God hates divorce, the Bible says. I also think that what God hates more than divorce is a toxic relationship.

The price you pay for remaining in an unhealthy and toxic relationship is too expensive.

Walk away from a lingering toxic relationship. Or, create a healthy distance while you both invest in long-term individual as well as marriage therapy. Give yourselves time to build your emotional intelligence and develop the necessary skills to allow yourselves to break out of the toxic behavior patterns. View counseling as an investment. Also, invest in good material on healthy communication in marriage.

As you are doing all of this, put your hope in God!

*To check or not to check?* I realized that my continuous snooping exposed me to details that caused me deep, long-term, self-inflicted emotional trauma. So, in my opinion, monitoring your partner's phone and social media accounts does more harm than good. What I discovered was that snooping quickly evolves into an addiction in itself. When you don't find anything, it compels you even the more, to keep looking. And if you discover something 'incriminating', your brain initially feels rewarded with feelings of validation in the knowledge that you weren't imagining things after all. But that is followed by unnecessary pain because of what you read.

Plus it's not your phone! I just believe that people should not snoop through their spouse's phone. I also think that the line "I was totally minding my own business when I noticed that his/her phone was beeping…" is rarely the full story. The full story often involves the fact that you had your eye on your spouse's phone and you were looking for even the slightest excuse to check.

The truth is that just the inkling that your spouse is inappropriately close to someone else, is already all the information you need to understand that your relationship has issues that you must attend to; before it goes into crisis. And, in my opinion, this holds true whether you spouse is 'escaping' from the marriage through a romantic liaison, through drugs or alcohol, or through spending long hours and an over-involvement in work or church or social or leisure activities. Please note that it doesn't mean that your spouse is doing these things because of anything you have done. But it does mean that, together, you must address your issues. Do invest in counseling, to get to the heart of the issue, and to learn how to communicate with each other

I learned that the true measure of a man is where he stands in times of controversy and conflict. I learned to not just accept the challenges and embarrassing failures in my life as a part of my history, but to OWN my story, and to applaud my resilience.

When we go through difficult things in life, it's tempting to lose hope that things will improve. And yes, there are many whose stories did not unfold like ours did. But God is in your story. He is still on His throne and He will bring you to a better place. God is bringing you through a tunnel and there is light at the end of that tunnel.

I titled this chapter *The Tunnel* because I was inspired by a profound piece written by my friend Natasha Nyanin:

"...If I begin to recount what I've been through in the last twelve months, you'd call it a melodrama of Shakespearean proportion, so I shall not. Still, I wasn't cast into a cave, I was going through a tunnel...Some tunnels are longer than others; this one more serpentine than that. But the thing I know about tunnels – having been through my longest, darkest one 5 years ago – is that tunnels, however obsidian, unlike caves, open up on the other side to a world of new and infinite possibilities..."

And so our journey continues…

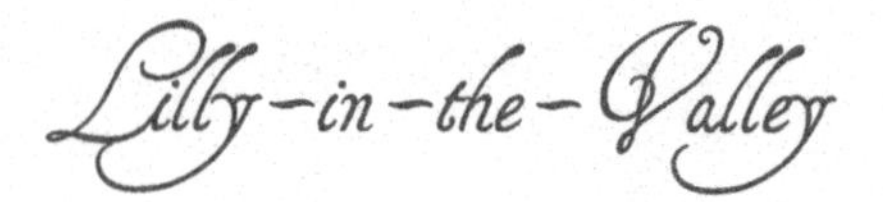

**(Facebook post, December 2017)**

**"He didn't have to hit me to leave a scar." – Allison M. Rockwell**

**"Awarebɔne tete ntoma." (A bad marriage destroys) – Akan proverb**

~~~~~~~~~~~~~~~~~~~~~~~~~~~~~~

I have been friends with my warrior-woman sister-friend Lilly for more than thirty years. 'Lilly' is actually not my sister-friend's real name. The meaning of her real name is 'flower' so I'll call her 'Lilly' in this essay.

As college students Lilly and I would spontaneously take road trips, try out new recipes and talk about our dreams. The world was our oyster and we planned to live life to the full.
~~~~~~~~~~~~~~~~~~~~~~~~~~~~~~

One thing that was evident about Lilly even then: she always had a very clear vision and goals for her life. And, with more focused determination than I had seen in anyone at our age, Lilly set out to achieve them.

Unsurprisingly, today Lilly has achieved every one of those mega-goals: a terminal degree, a senior management position with a large reputable organization, a beautiful family and a wonderful church family, where she is a ministry leader. And with all of these responsibilities, Lilly still manages to make time for her athletics and rocks the same figure she had thirty years ago!

As the years rolled by, Lilly and I had settled in different countries and unfortunately stayed in touch less frequently; our excuse being the pressures of marriage, motherhood and careers.

Facebook was helpful; a comment here, a 'like' there. To me, Lilly's life was picture perfect and I was incredibly proud of her.

A couple of years ago, Lilly called me on the phone in response to a Facebook post I had made. That day, we stayed on the phone for a solid two hours. An hour of that was Lilly just sobbing. That was when our sister-bond truly re-established.

Shortly afterwards we made plans to meet. My lasting impression from that reunion? Lilly's eyes looked sad and soulless.

A few months ago, Lilly called me and asked me to write her story anonymously. My response to her was that I would write it only when it felt "right".

Why? Because Lilly's story is still unfolding. In fact, as I write, there is not a grand Hollywood-style climactic victory to report. Lilly is going through a very difficult time. She is battling depression, regret and confusion.

However, in the wake of 2017's #OrangeTheWorld campaign, that seeks to end violence against women, I decided that today would be good day to write about a common but little-recognized type of Domestic Violence.

Friends, my sister-friend Lilly is a survivor of Psychological Abuse. Psychological abuse is insidious and toxic. And often not acknowledged.

One in three women worldwide endures some form of abuse, so Lilly's story is unfortunately not unique. Therefore, if you are reading this, either you or someone close to you is being abused psychologically.

The purpose of my post is purely to educate. I'm not looking to put out salacious details and I'm definitely not looking to male-bash. I'm simply asking that you who are reading – whatever your gender – please read to the end, WITH AN OPEN MIND. And then take the messages I have shared here to shine a light against your own behaviors. WITHOUT ANY DEFENSIVENESS.

And then please, please, PLEASE make any necessary changes. There is a wealth of resources out there to help you.

Too many marriages and families are suffering as a result of psychological and verbal abuse. A major reason is that so many of us were raised in the midst of unhealthy behaviors.

Also, just because certain ways of communication may be the norm of one's culture or may have been what you witnessed from your environment growing up doesn't make it right. If you stick to a behavior *just because* it has been the "Ghanaian" way or your "family's way", then you do yourself and your loved ones a gross injustice.

Here's one instant red flag you should be aware of for yourself – that you read this post and are simply dismissive of it.

In life, when we know better, we do better. So please educate yourself. Challenge your conventions. Change your world.

Lilly and her husband are attractive people and great conversationalists. Not some 'crazy' looking couple. They are active in their church. Lilly doesn't fit into the traditional "abused woman" stereotype. She is well educated, financially independent, a go-getter in life and someone who is actually incredibly confident in many other areas of her life. That is part of the reason why Lilly was in denial about her situation for so many years.

Are you still reading? Then you owe it to yourself to also read up on the manipulation tactics used in psychological abuse. Educate yourself on concepts such as intimidation, shifting the focus, minimizing, invalidation, scapegoating, belittling, gas lighting, guilt, shame, blame, silent treatment and several more.

Unfortunately, even the best of us exhibit some of these behaviors, often unknowingly. Or we do it, but justify these behaviors.

There is never any justification for psychological abuse!

Again, I'm not here to label or shame anyone. I'm asking you to honestly assess yourself based on what you will read below, and honestly determine whether you display even some of these unhealthy behaviors.

I want you to understand that these behaviors literally kill your spouse's soul. And I'm asking you to please make changes before it is too late.

Lilly is blessed with a strong family support system. For years, her sisters had picked up on what was going on and had tried to warn her. For years Lilly was in denial, but they loved her and stood by her till she was ready for change.

When Lilly asked me to tell her story, I posed a few questions to Lilly and her sisters and asked them to respond to me in writing. So, in telling Lilly's story, all I will be doing below is presenting direct quotes from Lilly and her sisters.

Before I do that, Lilly, I want to tell you that I love you. You are one of the strongest women I know. Never have you been weak through all of this. You are an overcomer!

And Lilly, don't worry. Stop crying about the past. Look forward to a good future. Remember what the Bible said, Lilly:

"Therefore I say to you, do not worry about your life...Consider the lilies of the field, how they grow: they neither toil nor spin..." – Matthew 6:25, 28 NKJV

~~~~~~~~~~~~~~~~~~~~~~~~~
~~~~~~~~~~~~~~~~~~~~~~~~~

Lilly's quotes:

"I shifted into 'I don't fail' mode and marriage was not something I wanted to fail in. I felt I might disappoint everyone."

"When something would happen and I would try to talk about it, we would spend hours with him running me around in circles. Sometimes, we would go so off tangent that the argument turned to something totally irrelevant or went way off topic. I would get so frustrated and stop."

"...If I insist and am still making my point and he knows I'm right, he gets angry. Or he'll tell me I don't know what I'm talking about. That he knows what he's saying, that he thinks before he speaks so I pretty much have no basis for any point I'm making."

"He yelled at me a lot. After I told him many times that if he yells I don't listen so if he wants me to listen, to speak to me nicely. Eventually he eased up on that, but then would ignore me often. And not speak to me for days or weeks if I said something to contradict him."

"If I had to discuss something with him or tell him I was going somewhere, I would rehearse what I was going to say for several days...preparing for what he might say. I have on a few occasions and even now, caught myself doing it and have to mentally tell myself it's ok."

"I would catch myself, if I was watching TV or speaking with my sisters, as soon as I hear him coming home I will quickly get off the phone or switch off the TV."

"Abuse is what I THOUGHT happened to other people, not me...I KNOW better, I'm smart, confident, strong...never me. But abuse eats away at you so so so slowly that your hands are in scorching water and you don't even realize it. THAT is how I felt. It's by the Grace of God that my eyes opened."

"How do you mentally recover and learn to trust anyone and believe anyone again? I'm always now listening to people and analyzing their behaviors and thinking..."

"And you know the scary thing???? I'm still sometimes doubting my brain whether what I'm saying is all true or my mind and feelings are playing tricks on me, wanting to believe what I've read is what I lived. It's insane. Meanwhile my examples are specific. And not made up. Gosh!! What a number on the brain. Oh, Aba, I'm reliving all this pain."

"He was very angry, yelled and swore at me and accused me. These scenarios were frequent in guilt-tripping me..."

"Everything seemed to be the opposite of what he says/does and he ALWAYS tried to turn things around on me, no matter what or how much I tried to reason or explain."

"With regards to his work schedule, I believe he used this to make sure I was always saddled with the kids and could never have a social life or 'alone' time."

"He would often neglect me or give me 'silent treatment'."

"... he turned this around and began saying 'my family was interfering in our marriage and taking too much of my time'. No amount of explanation got through to him. I always had a gut feeling that he wanted to make sure I had no social outlet besides the kids, him and maybe work."

"I have a very close family and because he could not succeed in isolating me from them, he began hating them and told his friends he did so – especially my sisters – because "they were putting ideas in my head" each time I would try to stand up to his abusive behavior. "

"He installed a camera on the outside of the house. The real reason he got the camera installed was to spy on me..."

"He has on several occasions yelled at me in front of the kids, his friends, and at one time even told my sisters to "fuck off" in front of his friend. This was so emotionally draining, and I was extremely sad and stressed very often. When I try to tell him that was not right, he would get angrier at me."

"At one point I told his mother about how unhappy her son was making me; when she tried to talk to him, he told her I was a liar, implied I was a bad mother and wife and that he has been responsible for everything relating to the family. He denied EVER yelling at me or treating me badly. Later when I confronted him with this asking why he would say that, he said..."It's over now so forget it". He did this several times whenever she tried to get to the bottom of things or reason with him and eventually told me "I was trying to destroy the relationship between his mother and him" when I tell her things he was doing."

"He would often tell me: you are on the phone too much, when the only people I ever spoke to were my sisters. Eventually, he took all the phones away from upstairs under the pretense that it disturbed the kids. And, at one point, he blocked my best friend's number off the phone so she could not reach me."

"He ruined almost every celebratory event for me: my wedding, the baptism of my children... We never celebrated anniversaries or my birthday because, without fail, about 3-4 days before the day he would flare up at me for no reason, get us into a fight, then the mood will be sour."

"A couple of years ago I had to have surgery. During the pre-op stages, I was trying to tell him about the surgery...He walked away from me and said, "What does it have to do with me?" In my hurt, I asked my dad to drop me off at the hospital. On the day of the operation my dad noticed my husband was home and asked me why he was not taking me...I lied and told him because he was working. I know my dad knew I was lying."

"After the operation, when I got home to recover, I literally interrupted his TV watching one night after that surgery and lifted up my dress to show him my surgery bandages and stitches just to get his attention. He just looked at the bandage said "Oh" and turned away back to the TV. I was on my own as always."

"It felt like I could never do anything right or enough – no matter how much I tried or did. And he told me so…"

"I think that, for years, I perhaps slipped into a mild depression from stress of three children, demanding job, doing everything on my own, and enduring a miserable marriage. I was in "survival mode" for years. I have always been a strong person – at least on the outside and my tendency to cope is to buck down and get things done – I operated almost "mechanically" for several years to just keep myself and the kids afloat."

"I told him one evening that I was very unhappy in the marriage and we need to make serious changes. He literally turned his back to me and ignored me for two weeks. After that time, I approached him again and told him same. This time he said what he usually says to project or try to make me second-guess or doubt myself, "We are both adults and know what we need to do...so if you do what you need to do, I'll do what I need to do and we are good". In the past, I would feel confused and wonder – how the conversation ended up here and how is it always my fault."

"He has never apologized for anything in twenty years because he said he only says sorry if he means it."

"Although I had read a few articles on abusive relationships, nothing clicked until I began doing more specific reading...and it all began making sense. I began connecting the dots with my experiences...that was when I began seeing the first psychologist to help me properly define this feeling and patterns I had experienced. It has been an absolute eye opener."

"I have overheard him on the phone many times doing the same smear - slandering my name and reputation - telling people what a two-faced wicked person I was; that I'm making him pay me (meaning I've asked him to now contribute to his upkeep and that of his children) that I'm basically a whore...and many other nasty things."

~~~~~~~~~~~~~~~~~~~~~~~~~
~~~~~~~~~~~~~~~~~~~~~~~~~

Quotes from Lilly's four sisters:

"The very first memory I have of his Jekyll and Hyde behavior was the day after your wedding. I must admit I was shocked. The way in which he spoke to you – yelled at you – in front of everyone with such a HARSH tone... I'd never heard or seen that side of him. Then it just continued...the way he would snap at you, the way you would say you shouldn't do this or that, and the way you would always tell us to "just leave it" or "it's ok". That was not the way we were raised. This was not you. And I feel like that is how he acted with you – you were doing well, good job, you took care of EVERYTHING, including him and I think he resented that and tried every which way to break you down."

"...Trying to drive a wedge between us, temper flaring for things that didn't make sense, the silent treatments to make everyone uncomfortable, the way he would talk to you so harshly over inconsequential things, the skewed way he acted towards you (absence of affection and over-abundance of blame)."

"But then there was also your behavior: You never went out, you rarely had fun, we would go out to do things and you were never "allowed" to do so, he would talk to you in that harsh tone and you would take it."

"I remember when I told you that you were my shero, but I didn't recognize you anymore. MY Lilly that I knew would have told him where to go and how to get there, but you seemed just sad and defeated for a long time. AND I also remember you responding something like 'Is it that obvious? I didn't think anyone could see that.'"

"Because of our mindset, 'abuse' was never really a consideration at first, because we thought 'that could never happen to us!'"

"But I remember reading one of those articles and recognizing SO many signs that I never would have pieced together had they not been right in front of me, and I thought maybe it would have the same effect on you.

"I think the saving grace in all this is that, in spite of ALL his efforts to isolate you, we were never going anywhere. If he had managed to separate you and your supports, I shudder to think of where we might be now..."

"Gosh...there are so many little things that seemed so...inconsequential at the time but, now stepping back, are so indicative of a deeper pattern."

"We – your sisters – sent you those articles because you stopped being yourself. We would often send them back and forth to each other and say, 'Do we send this one too?' All the signs were there. It was like a TV show – he would try to isolate you, you stopped seeing friends, you would defend his behavior and make it seem not so bad when clearly it was. I think you were lying to yourself."

"At the end of the day, you tried to bolster a person who is so broken and wounded that you allowed him to ALMOST break you too. Your kind heart did you in. But you are here now – you're getting back to yourself. For me, there is no greater joy than to see you start living again. Your true self is coming back. This was the worst of the abuse; that you lost yourself and lost your way. God is bringing you back; that is evident to all who see you now..."

~~~~~~~~~~~~~~~~~~~~~~~~

Lilly's Update:

Don't feel sorry for me, because the worst is over. It was damaging. But I can tell you that I am a living example of God's amazing and unfailing Grace.

Next time you hear or read about this type of abuse from anyone, just think of me. I NEVER ever thought it would ever be me. I'm too strong, too smart, too intelligent to be abused... but abuse does not discriminate.

Do keep the dialogue going. Maybe my story can save one more woman.
~~~~~~~~~~~~~~~~~~~~~~~~

I'm humbled by the amount of comments both public and private. When I told Aba I needed her help to get my story out, this is exactly what I had envisioned. I am glad I could touch one more person.

Lilly

## Even if you are Right

***A Christian couple inspired this piece. Despite their stated good intentions for their marriage and their family, they have not yet fully committed to the process of challenging and changing their dysfunctional patterns of behavior. As always, my sole purpose is to bring insight for positive change.***

**"Abufuo pamo adepa firi fie." (Anger drives something good from the house) – Akan proverb**

~~~~~~~~~~~~~~~~~~~~~~~~~~~

Even if you are right and they are wrong.

Even if you know what is best for them, but they can't see it. Even if you've told them something over and over again, yet they refuse to comply. Even if they irritate you with their response and their attitude...
~~~~~~~~~~~~~~~~~~~~~~~~~~~

Hear me well!!!!

You have NO RIGHT to be disrespectful, or to scream, or to hurl insults at them, or to call them names!

You have NO RIGHT to threaten them, get in their face, intimidate them, shove them, push them, bite them, scratch them, knock them, slap them, kick them or beat them!

You have NO RIGHT to give them intimidating looks or gestures, or to destroy their belongings!

You have NO RIGHT to manipulate them by withholding money they need to live, or by denying them access to the family income!

You have NO RIGHT to play mind games with them, or to belittle them, or to discredit their opinions, or to call them crazy!

Whoever you are - male or female - if you do a few of these things, or some of these things, or most of these things, then know that this is ABUSIVE behavior, and there is NO EXCUSE for that. Absolutely none! Nothing justifies abusive behavior!

Get professional help to learn how to manage your anger and to learn healthy ways to communicate.

Otherwise, sooner or later you WILL lose your loved ones!

# Dear Absentee Dad

***This piece was inspired by an absentee divorced Dad. However, the message holds true for all absentee parents. As always, my sole purpose is to bring insight for positive change.***

~~~~~~~~~~~~~~~~~~~~~~~~

Dear Absentee Dad,
After the bitter divorce, you moved away in anger and sorrow. You haven't seen your children in years. You contact them infrequently. Who will nurture and protect your children?

Dear Absentee Dad,
You have not been faithful in paying your child support. The best you do is to offer a little money "from time to time".
Do your children eat, "from time to time"?
Do they go to school, "from time to time"?
~~~~~~~~~~~~~~~~~~~~~~~~

Do they need a place to live, "from time to time"?

Dear Absentee Dad,
You have your version of the story you tell the world. Do you realize that your child, too, has her own memories of what she saw you say and do??

Dear Absentee Dad,
Do you know that your child sorely misses you? That she has been broken-hearted all these years?

Dear Absentee Dad,
Do you know that your child inherited your intellect? Your love of science and history? Your conviction? Your boldness?

Dear Absentee Dad,
Could you have predicted that one day your child would grow in great wisdom? And that one day she would find her voice?

Dear Absentee Dad,
Did you ever fathom, that in the fullness of time, your child would look you in the eye and call you out on your choices?

Dear Absentee Dad,
Could you have ever imagined this moment, when face-to face with your child, you had absolutely no defense? Because

what defense can there EVER be when a father financially and emotionally does not give his BEST to his children?

Dear Absentee Dad,
You are full of regrets now. Your despair cuts deep. You realized, too late, that being divorced from your wife should NEVER mean being divorced from your children.

~~~~~~~~~~~~~~~~~~~~~~~~

**"Baby, there ain't no mountain high enough**
**Ain't no valley low enough**
**Ain't no river wide enough**
**To keep me from you babe"**

*Performed by Marvin Gaye*
~~~~~~~~~~~~~~~~~~~~~~~~

# *Baby M*

"Where is death's sting? Where, grave thy victory? I triumph still, if Thou abide with me." – Henry Francis Lyte

"I have always believed, and I still believe, that whatever good or bad fortune may come our way we can always give it meaning and transform it into something of value." – Hermann Hesse

"You intended to harm me, but God intended it for good to accomplish what is now being done…" – Genesis 50:20

~~~~~~~~~~~~~~~~~~~~~~~~~~

*Baby M was my godson. He lived for six days. Within the short span of his life we experienced a full range of emotions; joy, disbelief, grief, worry, hope and ultimately,*
~~~~~~~~~~~~~~~~~~~~~~~~~~

*acceptance that it was most likely God's will that he wouldn't be with us for long. Upon finally realizing that we would not have much time with Baby M, we chose to cherish every moment we had with him. And so even through our tears, there was joy and laughter. We celebrated every victory as our little warrior valiantly fought for his life and we covered him in prayer during the difficult moments. At every turn, we were buoyed by the kindness and compassion of an excellent team of dedicated doctors, nurses, hospital chaplains and volunteers who went above and beyond the call of duty.*

I experienced some profound truths from this experience:

1. Every life has a divine purpose. That purpose unfolds moment by moment. Therefore, it's important to live fully in each moment. If we don't pay attention, we will miss much of what life has to teach us.

2. Life is indeed like a vapor – here today and gone tomorrow. The Bible says there is a time for mourning. When that time comes, we will mourn. Till then, let's fully celebrate life.

3. Life is precious, so let's not take it for granted. Let's hold our loved ones a little tighter and not miss a single opportunity to express our love to them.

4. Life will throw inexplicable curveballs our way. In time we may make some sense of it all. Till then, we will trust God.

5. Let's cling to hope. Hope really is our lifeline!

6. Compassion and thoughtfulness are powerfully healing forces! They really do bring light into dark moments. If you are reading this and you are one of those people who selflessly give of your time, your skill and your substance in compassionate ways and through anonymous acts of kindness, I salute you! You may never know whose life you've touched. But please know that you have. I pray God blesses you and rewards you richly!

# The Hard Slamming Door

**A rejection is nothing more than a necessary step in the pursuit of success." –*Bo Bennett***

**"We've been…battered by troubles, but we're not demoralized…" –2 Corinthians 4: 7-12 AMP**

**"Consider it a sheer gift, friends, when tests and challenges come at you from all sides. You know that under pressure, your faith-life is forced into the open and shows its true colors. So don't try to get out of anything prematurely. Let it do its work so you become mature and well-developed, not deficient in any way." – James 1:2-4 MSG**

~~~~~~~~~~~~~~~~~~~~~~~~~~

My friend Charles fell head over heels in love with a young lady. Not only was she beautiful and intelligent, but she also
~~~~~~~~~~~~~~~~~~~~~~~~~~

possessed all the attributes he desired in a woman. And their chemistry was unbelievable, Charles said. He very quickly became very attached to her and felt incredibly blessed to have found her. Within months, they began to make major preparations towards spending the rest of their lives together.

But one day, out of the blue, she abruptly ended the relationship. Charles felt blindsided. As far as he was concerned, their relationship had been blissful. They spent a lot of time together and she had never communicated that she had any misgivings about their relationship. He could not understand what had caused her drastic change of heart.

The breakup was swift and definitive; one day they had been planning a wedding, but by the next day she was completely out of his life. Charles was sorely tempted to beg her to stay, but he changed his mind with the realization that it was pointless to hold on to someone who didn't want to be with him.

So, with all the dignity he could muster, Charles wished her well and let her go.

In the aftermath of their breakup, Charles spiraled into shock, hurt and confusion. He had loved his lady wholeheartedly and had given her his absolute best. Charles' self-confidence plummeted. He wondered what was so wrong with him that she would leave him in that brutal manner.

A few weeks after the breakup, Charles realized that the young lady had gone back to her former fiancé. Now he really felt like a fool.

But in that vulnerable season of his life, grieving and feeling lost, Charles deepened his relationship with God. In time, he also began to deal with other longstanding issues and hurts in his life. He worked on rebuilding his self-esteem. He changed his diet and began to exercise. He went back to school. A year after the breakup, Charles had undergonc a pretty dramatic physical, spiritual and emotional transformation.

After a few years Charles found love again. He married an amazing wife and began to raise a beautiful family. He had moved on successfully.

And then, one day, out of the blue, Charles received a text message followed by a phone call from his ex-girlfriend. They had a friendly exchange and got caught up with the happenings in each other's lives. Life had been kind to her also. She had built a successful career, had a loving family and an abiding faith. During their ten-minute conversation, Charles noted that the easy rapport they had shared was still there. At the end of the conversation, she asked Charles if it would be possible to meet up with him in person. Charles suspected that she wanted to apologize so that she could finally get closure.

"Are you sure that meeting up with her is a really good idea?" I asked skeptically. Charles smiled in response, but what he said next gave me food for thought. Getting close to her again, on any level, was not an option for him, Charles said; not just because of the possible risk of temptation, but also because he knew that stepping back into their old dynamic could also risk him going back to the unhealthy dependency he'd had on her.

"It's not even about her, it's about me," Charles said. "Ten years ago, God allowed that door to close in my life. In fact, the door didn't just close; it slammed into my face. And although it hurt like hell, I now see that it had to happen. Because, that experience forced me to grow into the Purpose that God has for me. God was directing my steps through that difficult experience. And so, I will never reopen that door to my past because I simply refuse to undo the progress and the personal growth I've achieved over these past ten years. God has brought me too far for that."

Charles' insightful statement blew me away. There were several nuggets of profound life wisdom that I grasped onto. I recalled times in my own life when doors had slammed painfully in my face. Like Charles, I also see that the hand of

God had been guiding me the whole time; not just by opening doors of opportunity, but also by closing certain doors in my life.

A closed door is also God's way of guiding us onto a path that is better for us than the path we had originally been on. Disappointments and closed doors are part of God's way of directing us towards His purpose and plan. And His plan for our lives is always the best option for our lives.

As I continued to think about what Charles said and the experience he had endured, these questions also came to my mind:

*Why, if the door had to close, could it not just close gently? Was there a specific purpose to a hard slamming door in our lives?*

Yes, I do believe that there is a purpose to experiencing a hard slamming door in our lives. Sometimes, the only thing that gets our attention strongly enough to compel us to change course in life, is a hard slamming door. The hard slamming door is able to make us hit our rock bottom, where we then have no choice but to re-evaluate our lives and begin to do things differently.

If the door had been shut even a smidgeon more gently, the truth is that we might have stubbornly refused to change course and we would have continued to try every means possible to go through a door that was not God's divine plan for our lives. Only the powerful force of a hard slamming door would have been able to shift our course.

God directs our paths not only by opening doors but also by closing certain doors. In life, times will certainly come when we experience a hard slamming door – that person you loved, who broke up with you; that promotion you worked so hard for, but didn't get; the beloved friend or trusted colleague who betrayed you; that financial hardship you endured; that debilitating sickness or injury that caused a radical transformation in your life…

The crushing disappointment of the hard slamming door, and the resulting change that comes about in our lives, is not an easy or fun process. Given the choice, who would choose to experience crushing defeats or stinging rejections or the searing pain of a hard slamming door? But, in the fullness of time, having grown through our "hard slamming door" experiences, God having healed our pain, we will look back with nothing but pure gratitude and declare, "Wow, God was indeed directing my paths all along!"

# "I Don't Want To Be Free!"

**"The secret of change is to focus all of your energy not on fighting the old, but on building the new." – Socrates**

**"Change is inevitable. Growth is optional." – John Maxwell**

~~~~~~~~~~~~~~~~~~~~~~~~~~

My daughter Elissa has always loved school. She is the only child I know of who would cry at the end of the school year and then be excited when school started.

Elissa particularly enjoyed her middle school years. A big reason for this was Mrs. Fontaine, the teacher who ran the ITV (Instructional Television) program at the school.

Every school morning, for three years, Elissa had the chance to film, direct, produce, edit and write scripts for her school's
~~~~~~~~~~~~~~~~~~~~~~~~~~

daily news program. She loved the challenge, the creativity and even the sacrifice of having to go to school early every day to work on these projects. Mrs. Fontaine created an ITV Team that was top notch technically, creatively and also had a genuine team spirit.

Elissa bloomed in that environment. Mrs. Fontaine was her teacher, mentor, cheerleader and friend rolled into one. I think what made their bond even more special was the fact that they are birthday twins.

Every child should experience a teacher like Mrs. Fontaine, who inspires them to be their best.

High school was a major transition for Elissa. Her closest friends had gone to different high schools and she particularly missed starting her day with her beloved "Mrs. Fontaine and the ITV crew".

But soon after the school year began, Elissa and her best friend, who had also been a member of their old ITV team, began volunteering after school on some of Mrs Fontaine's projects. Whenever they got together, it was just like old times and Elissa always seemed energized after those visits.

I thought it was wonderful that Elissa was maintaining those cherished friendships, but it seemed to me that what she was also trying to do was to keep the past alive. Because of that focus, it was taking her longer to feel settled in her new school, and to fully embrace new friendships.

Elissa's heart still seemed to be in her old middle school.

One day, Elissa announced to me that Mrs. Fontaine was moving on to a fantastic new opportunity at a different school. I realized that the news had hit Elissa hard, so I decided that it was a good time to voice out my suspicion to her.

"Elissa," I said, "I know you've really enjoyed going back to your old school to volunteer with Mrs. Fontaine. But perhaps Mrs. Fontaine moving on is a blessing for you as well. Without those visits to fall back on, maybe now you can be free to fully embrace your new school and all that it has to offer."

"BUT I DON'T WANT TO BE FREE!!!" she burst out.

With that statement, I knew we had hit the heart of the matter. Elissa wasn't yet ready to let go of middle school.

As a child I owned an illustrated book of Bible stories for children. I remember one of the illustrations depicting the scene from the bible story of a man called Lot and his family fleeing the city of Sodom as it began to rain fire and brimstone.

The account of how Lot and his family fled from Sodom is found in Genesis chapter 19. God sent two angels to warn Lot and his family to leave Sodom quickly, because destruction was going to hit the city. In fact, because they were hesitating, the angels actually grabbed Lot and his family by their wrists and rushed them to safety outside the city gates. The angels' instructions were "do not look behind you or stop anywhere in the entire valley...or you will be consumed and swept away".

As they ran towards their new life, however, the Bible states that Lot's wife "foolishly, longingly looked back...in an act of disobedience" (Genesis 19:26 AMP). And because of this became a pillar of salt.

I can still picture that illustration from my Children's Bible book; the salt figure of a woman looking back, rooted to the same spot, even as the rest of her family ran towards their future.

I was always curious as to why Lot's wife turned into a pillar of salt. Bible scholars have proffered various explanations as to why she was "punished by salt". I wondered what other insights and wisdom were imbedded in that story.

Among its many uses, salt is a preservative. For example, salt is used widely in food preservation, notably in salted fish and cured meats.

Given the preservative property of salt, could there also be a figurative meaning in the story of Lot's wife turning into a pillar of salt because she looked back?

Were there things in Sodom that Lot's wife was reluctant to leave behind? Perhaps a beautiful home? Valuable material possessions? A vibrant social life? It's hard to move on from a past that was filled with good things.

Or did the reality that the family had left behind all of their material possessions in Sodom and were going to start life all over again hit her so hard, that it compelled her to pause and look back?

Or did she look back in grief and mourning because her daughters' fiancés had refused to flee with them, disbelieving that Sodom was really going to be destroyed?

Or could it have been, perhaps, that Lot's wife had herself participated in the depravity in Sodom, and was filled with such shame at her past choices that she could not resist looking back with regret?

Disclaimer: I don't know what prompted Lot's wife to look back. I offered these possible scenarios using artistic license, rather than as a Bible expert.

The lesson I picked from the story of Lot's wife is that, literally and figuratively, by "foolishly" looking back and not allowing herself to let go of her past, she was unable to move on to the future that awaited her. She died, an unmovable pillar of salt; stuck to her past.

Change is unavoidable in our lives. The Greek philosopher Heraclitus said, "The only thing constant is change". The Bible states: "There is a season (a time appointed) for everything and a time for every...event or purpose under heaven." – Ecclesiastes 3:1AMP

As different events, activities, milestones and rites of passage unfold in our lives, we inevitably WILL transition into different seasons of our lives.

It's not always easy to embrace new seasons in our lives. Like my daughter Elissa, it may be hard to let go of someone or something or some place that we love. Yet it's important to allow ourselves to move on to our new season, knowing that the cherished memories will forever be etched in our hearts.

Even in situations where the past was dysfunctional or unpleasant, it still may be hard to let go, because that was all we knew. Change is often scary, just because we are afraid of the unknown.

Thankfully, whatever our past, through every changing season in our lives, we have a God who is unchanging and faithful. That is something we should never, ever forget!

~~~~~~~~~~~~~~~~~~~~~~~~~

Be still, my soul; the Lord is on thy side;
Bear patiently the cross of grief or pain;
Leave to thy God to order and provide;
In every change He faithful will remain.
Be still, my soul; thy best, thy heavenly, Friend
Through thorny ways leads to a joyful end.

Be still, my soul; thy God doth undertake
To guide the future as He has the past.
Thy hope, thy confidence, let nothing shake;
All now mysterious shall be bright at last.
Be still, my soul; the waves and winds still know
His voice who ruled them while He dwelt below.

*Lyrics from the hymn "Be Still My Soul" by Catharina von Schlegel*
~~~~~~~~~~~~~~~~~~~~~~~~~

# The Elegant Surgeon

**"Who shall separate us from the love of Christ? – Romans 8:35 NIV**

**"Biribiara nni hɔ a ɛkwati Nyame." (There is no single thing that can by-pass God) – Akan proverb**

~~~~~~~~~~~~~~~~~~~~~~~~~~~~

A dear sister-friend of mine, an amazing, faith-filled, charismatic, loving human being, recently received a health diagnosis that altered her life, as she knew it. As a result of this diagnosis, her career had to come to an immediate end.

My sister-friend is a surgeon, well-loved by her grateful patients and well respected by her peers. A colleague of hers once described her surgical skills as "elegant". So my nickname for her became 'Elegant Surgeon'.
~~~~~~~~~~~~~~~~~~~~~~~~~~~~

Up until she got the news, Elegant Surgeon had no reason not to look forward to many more vibrant years of a thriving career and her happy home life. Sadly though, disease was lurking deep in her DNA; silently waiting to rear its head.

I was shaken when I heard the news. I took my frayed emotions to God.

Me: Lord?
God: Yes, my child?
Me: My heart is heavy.
God: Talk to me.
Me: Why, Father? Why did you do this to Elegant Surgeon?
God: I didn't DO this to Elegant Surgeon. I don't bring bad things on people. I only bring good things and perfect gifts.
Me: You know what I mean, Father. Why did you allow this sickness to happen to somebody so brilliant and who is such a good person?
God: Are you saying that someone who is less of a good person and less brilliant than Elegant Surgeon is somehow more deserving of sickness?
Me: That's not what I meant, Father. Let me rephrase that: *doesn't it seem like so much talent will be going to waste*?
God: Her surgical talent was a gift I gave her. It was for a season. And during that season she used her gifts to serve my people very well. I am well pleased with my daughter.
Me: I still don't get it. It's not fair, Father.
God: Who ever said life was fair? Show me one person who

complained when they were recipients of my extraordinary grace.

Me: <Sigh>. Ok, Lord, I get that part. But Father, why her?

God: Why not her?

Me: What did she do to deserve this suffering?

God: <Silence>

Me: Don't you love her enough to heal her right now, so that we can all just forget that today ever happened? Huh?

God: <Silence>

Me: Why won't you answer me, Father?

God: I'm speaking child, but you cannot hear from me when you are filled with such anger and wrong ideas about this situation and about Me.

Me: <Sigh>...Okay, speak now Lord, I am listening.

God: "Can anything ever separate us from Christ's love? Does it mean He no longer loves us if we have trouble or calamity, or are persecuted, or hungry, or destitute, or in danger, or threatened with death? No, despite all these things, overwhelming victory is ours through Christ, who loved us. And I am convinced that nothing can ever separate us from God's love. Neither death nor life, neither angels nor demons, neither our fears for today nor our worries about tomorrow – not even the powers of hell can separate us from God's love. No power in the sky above or in the earth below – indeed, nothing in all creation will ever be able to separate us from the love of God that is revealed in Christ Jesus our Lord." – Romans 8:35, 37-39 NLT

Me: So, you still love her, Lord?

God: As much as I ever have!

Me: And you are still with her, Lord?
God: I won't abandon her, nor will I ever fail her.
Me: It's a long road ahead for her, Lord.
God: "My Grace is sufficient for her..."

**Lord, I offer my life to You**
Everything I've been through
Use it for Your glory
Lord I offer my days to You
Lifting my praise to You
As a pleasing sacrifice
Lord I offer You my life

Only By Grace

# “*Chapter 49*”

**(October 9, 2018)**

**“Mental Health is … critical to wellbeing.” – Diane Abbot**

**“Why are you in despair, O my soul? …Hope in God…” – Psalm 42: 5-6**

~~~~~~~~~~~~~~~~~~~~~~~~~~

The past year saw me blessed with unprecedented blessings and exciting new projects. But, in all honesty, more than in any other period I can recall over the past decade, this past year was also marked by change, challenge and uncomfortable growth.

My initial heady rush of excitement slowly gave way to uncertainty as my brain swung into overdrive; asking myself questions like, *What if it all fails?*, *What if…?*
~~~~~~~~~~~~~~~~~~~~~~~~~~

Before long, "uncertainty" invited "overwhelmed" to become a roommate in my headspace.

On the outside, I acted like my usual self, but the truth was that my mind continually churned with worry about everything and everyone in my life.

Soon, I could no longer deny the fact that a "bit of worry" had evolved into a pervasive fear that sapped my energy and robbed me of my joie de vivre.

I have always been fascinated by observing young children at play. I love their carefree, boundless energy and their innate ability to savor the present moment, unencumbered by worry. The joy in children is pure, unfettered and totally infectious, because joy is their default state.

I believe that all human beings are born with joyfulness as our default state. That is, until the cares of the world – fear of change, tragedy, trauma, abuse, illness, loss, betrayals, life stressors of all sorts – come into our lives to discomfit, deflate, demoralize, strangle and eventually strip us of joy. And then, sadly, joy is no longer our default state. Which means we must fight to maintain our joy.

My fight has been a multi-pronged approach. I'm being intentional to give my body the balanced nutrition it needs so that I can accomplish the Purposes for which I was created. I'm also trying to consistently get moderate exercise.

I'm being mindful to center my attention on positive, encouraging, life-affirming thoughts and affirmations. I am carefully choosing the material I read or listen to, and the people I allow into my inner circle.

I've significantly limited my social media use, to allow me to better manage my time, but also as a deliberate strategy to avoid the well-documented mental health risks that can be caused by excessive social media use.

I take a couple of minutes every day to be still and just breathe. I find that to be an excellent practice. Sunrises make me happy and also remind me of God's faithfulness. So, I try to go walking and watch the sun rise as often as I can.

A major part of my fight has involved growing in my faith. One thing I learned about myself is that I get anxious when I try to go at a different pace than God's perfect timing. And I definitely feel anxious when I stray outside of His perfect will for my life. So, I'm learning to wait on God and to surrender myself to His perfect plan for my life. I take on life one day at a time. And He always gives me new strength for the next day.

This is my journey to rebuilding my joy, my faith and my resilience.

I do this because I owe it to myself and to my loved ones to be the highest, truest expression of myself. And so, every day, I press on, knowing that my unchanging God is my anchor through my changing seasons.

Today, I confidently begin Chapter 49 – my fiftieth year of life – with these words as my anthem:

Sing praise my soul, find strength in Joy
Let His Words lead you on
Do not forget, His great faithfulness
He'll finish all He's begun
So take courage my heart, stay steadfast my soul
He's in the waiting, He's in the waiting
Hold onto your hope, as your triumph unfolds
He's never failing, He's never failing
And You who hold the stars; Who call them each by name
Will surely keep Your promise to me
That I will rise, in Your victory…

*From the song "Take Courage" by Bethel Music*

Post script:
If you are reading this, then I'm 100% sure that you have felt overwhelmed or sad or fearful at some period in your life.

Or perhaps, you've been trying unsuccessfully to fight back against a chronic low-grade depression or anxiety.

The World Health Organization (WHO) reports that one in four people will be affected by a mental disorder during the course of their lifetimes; so if you're still reading this, chances are that either you or a loved one has been affected by a mental disorder like Major Depressive Disorder, an Anxiety Disorder, Bipolar Disorder and more.

If so, please fight back to regain your best self!

Fight back through getting healthy nutrition, moderate exercise, meditation and building your faith.

Fight back by talking to someone you trust. Psychotherapy with a mental health professional is an excellent investment in yourself.

Sometimes this fight may require taking medication prescribed by your physician. If so, take your medicine as prescribed.

Fight to become the highest and truest expression of yourself.

Fight to maintain your mental health. There is no shame in talking about your mental health.

There is no health without mental health!

"Dear friend, I pray that you may enjoy good health and that all may go well with you, even as your soul is getting along well." – 3 John 1:2 NIV

# His Gentleness Has Made Me Great

**(October 9, 2016)**

**"The Lord is ... is patient toward you." – 2 Peter 3:9**

**"Be gentle with yourself...keep peace in your soul." – Max Ehrman**

**"Be careful how you are talking to yourself, because you are listening." – Lisa Hayes**

~~~~~~~~~~~~~~~~~~~~~~~~~~~

Okay, so it's actually the 20th anniversary of my 27th birthday, but who is counting?

At 47, what do I know for sure? That God has been incredibly patient with me. And that daily He continues to gently mold me into the greatness He created me to be.
~~~~~~~~~~~~~~~~~~~~~~~~~~~

In 47 years, I've had disappointments. I have been disappointing. Each time God picks me up, comforts me, disciplines me lovingly where necessary, and then sets me back on my path.

In my 47 years, I have truly come to identify with David, when he said this of God: "Your gentleness has made me great." (Psalms 18:35)

I remember as a little girl I had thick, kinky hair. It was a nightmare to comb. And my mother would scold me whenever she caught me 'fighting' with my hair. I remember her always saying "You are not gentle with your hair at all!"

And for many years of my life, I was not gentle with myself either. I was constantly hypercritical of myself. Constantly trying to appear perfect. Constantly seeking the approval of others.

At 47, I am glad to say that I'm finally getting the hang of being gentle with myself.

I don't take God's gentleness for granted. What reassurance it has been to know that my gentle and patient God is always by my side, every step of the way!

Every day and in every way, may His gentleness make you great!

## *Spoiler Alert*
(October 9, 2017)

**"Onyankopon adom nti, biribiara bɛyɛ yie." - an Adinkra symbol of the Akans of Ghana, which translated, means: "By God's grace, all will be well."[7]**

**"Obisabisafoɔ nto [mfom/kwan]." (One who asks the way does not lose the road). - Akan proverb**

~~~~~~~~~~~~~~~~~~~~~~~~~~

On my birthday this week, my son Archie said to me: "Mom, at 48 do you realize that you've probably lived most of your life already?!"

My response: "Maybe, but my best years are still ahead of me, son!"

[7] Willis, W. Bruce. The Adinkra dictionary: a visual primer of the language of the Adinkra. Washington, D. C.: Pyramid Complex, 1998.
~~~~~~~~~~~~~~~~~~~~~~~~~~

My answer was smooth, but it did make me reflective: can I really say that my best years are still ahead of me?

I had a great year. My family is wonderful. And this year, new and exciting opportunities opened up in my life.

But the year was also peppered with challenges: Health concerns. My decision to distance myself from a loved one's toxic behavior. My disillusionment at the state of the world.

Every year, I ask God for a special message on my birthday, to encourage me for the year ahead.

This year I got my message through an amazing conversation I had with a wise friend of mine. My friend had a heart attack a few weeks ago. Thanks to excellent medical intervention, he survived. But he came extremely close to dying.

I asked him what he experienced in the moments that his life hung in the balance. He answered that he saw himself traveling over a beautiful green meadow. Somehow my friend knew that when he got to the end of the meadow, there would be a hole in the ground for his grave. He said he felt a profound, incredible, beautiful sense of peace.

My friend was blessed to have experienced a taste of eternity. It was a glorious feeling like no other. Now, he says he has no fear of the future.

I understand why that is. As a child I was an avid reader, but often the suspense in the story would be too much for me to bear, so I was big on 'spoilers'. Whenever I began reading a new book, I would flip to the back page to find out what happened at the end. Once I had read the end of the book, with the assurance that the story would end well, I could then go on to read the whole book without feeling nervous.

The thing about this life is that we've been given a bunch of 'spoilers' in the Bible. Because He lives, we now have Life. Because He overcame, we will overcome! Because of the many 'spoilers' found in the Word of God, we can indeed live our lives without fear.

My friend also said that, before his heart attack, his prayers were often requests to God to take care of things in his life. Now he says that his prayer life has been transformed to the point where a lot of his prayers are simply, "God, draw me close to You." You see, he now knows, beyond a shadow of a doubt, that as long as he sticks close to God, everything will be all right.

With that, I received my birthday message: “Don't get hung up on the ups and downs of life, Aba. Just stay close to Me. It's the only thing you need!"

With all that life may bring, I pray that life will never ever keep you down. Stick close to God. With Him by your side, your best days are surely ahead.!

~~~~~~~~~~~~~~~~~~~~~~~~~~

I have won
and I have lost
I got it right sometimes
But sometimes I did not
Life's been a journey
I've seen joy, I've seen regret
Oh and You have been my God
Through all of it...
*(From 'Through All of It' by Colton Dixon)*

Draw me close to you
Never let me go
I lay it all down again
To hear you say that I'm your friend
You are my desire
No one else will do
'Cause nothing else can take your place
To feel the warmth of your embrace
Help me find the way
Bring me back to you
You're all I want
You're all I've ever needed
You're all I want
Help me know you are near...
*(From 'Draw Me Close' by Michael W. Smith)*
~~~~~~~~~~~~~~~~~~~~~~~~~~

## *Just Remember*

**"O Lord, I remember Your name in the night." – Psalm 119:55**

~~~~~~~~~~~~~~~~~~~~~~~~~~~~

The day itself, almost 30 years ago, was remarkably unremarkable. In fact, the only thing I remember about that day was the Near-Incident.

I was a university student, majoring in Biochemistry. It was a period where I was starting to re-think my intended career path in science, because I had realized that I just didn't enjoy doing lab work.

That afternoon, I was doing a chemistry experiment in the lab; frankly, at that moment, wishing I could be anywhere else in the world but in the lab. I needed to rinse off my
~~~~~~~~~~~~~~~~~~~~~~~~~~~~

glassware, so I robotically picked up a bottle of distilled water that was at a nearby station and took it to the sink...

As a big splash of liquid hit the wet sink, the bigger 'whoosh' of effervescence made it abundantly clear to me that I had made a terrible mistake.

It turned out that the bottle in my hand did not in fact contain distilled water, but Aqua Regia, a highly concentrated and corrosive acid that is supposed to be handled with protective gear, including lab coat, safety goggles and acid-resistant gloves. None of which I was wearing!

I set the bottle down in shock, as the magnitude of what had just happened began to dawn on me. Even though I had been careless, NOT A DROP of acid had splashed on my hands, or my skin, or my eyes, or my clothes!!! Nor was there any property damage.

The outcome could have been very, very different.

It was a humbling experience for me. It is one incident in my life where I experienced the pure Mercy of God, despite my shortcomings.

There have since been many, many occasions in my life when I have experienced the mercy, the deliverance, the protection, the compassion, the goodness, and the favor of

God. Often in spite of a mess I created. Sometimes, I was the innocent party. And other times, it was no one's fault; life just happened. Sometimes, God disciplined me, but ALWAYS I emerged stronger and wiser…

The constant theme in my life has been God's faithfulness. He has always taken care of me and mine, even when I couldn't see it.

So, I memorialize all of my stories; I never allow myself to forget. I do this because it keeps me grateful and gives me hope for the future. It fills me with confidence to know that the same God who protected this careless 21-year-old from major acid burns, will continue to be right by her side, throughout her life.

My Gratitude is my major armament against entitlement, complacency and depression.

My Gratitude helps me to shift my focus from my circumstances, however dire they may appear, to the greatness of my God.

There was a young man I read about called Jacob. He was quite the manipulator. In a story with more drama than any Hollywood movie, Jacob betrayed his older twin brother, Esau and stole his birthright. Esau was understandably furious and planned to kill Jacob.

So, Jacob fled from his land, towards a very uncertain future, and possibly with some regret at what he had done to his brother. On the journey, he stopped for the night, and went to sleep, placing a stone under his head. That was when he had a most spectacular dream of a staircase leading to heaven, with angels going up and down the staircase. And then Jacob saw God himself, who reassured him that he would be fine, and that his life would go on, according to God's amazing plan. This is what God said to Jacob in the dream:

“Behold, I am with you and will keep you wherever you go, and will bring you back to this land; for I will not leave you until I have done that of which I have spoken to you." Then Jacob awoke from his sleep and said, "Surely the Lord is in this place; and I did not know it." (Genesis 28:15-16 NJKV)

The dream was so spectacular that Jacob knew that he could not afford to forget. He built a memorial at that spot.

That's what I do too. I build a memorial whenever I recall all the good things God has done in my life. My gratitude is my memorial. By just remembering the things God has done in my life, it powerfully serves to remind me that surely, God is still working in my life and circumstances. And I am reassured that my life WILL go according to the amazing plan He has for me.

My gratitude is indeed my not-so-secret weapon.

Let's make it a point to remember our blessings and the things God has brought us through. And then watch the powerful effect of our Gratitude begin to manifest in our lives.

Just Remember!

~~~~~~~~~~~~~~~~~~~~~~~~~

Count Your Blessings

When upon life's billows you are tempest-tossed,
When you are discouraged, thinking all is lost,
Count your many blessings, name them one by one,
And it will surprise you what the Lord has done.

Count your blessings, name them one by one,
Count your blessings, see what God has done!
Count your blessings, name them one by one,
And it will surprise you what the Lord has done

Are you ever burdened with a load of care?
Does the cross seem heavy you are called to bear?
Count your many blessings, every doubt will fly,
And you will keep singing as the days go by.

*Johnson Oatman Jr.*
~~~~~~~~~~~~~~~~~~~~~~~~~

# Testimony of an Irma-gee

**(September 13, 2017)**

**"When you come out of the storm, you won't be the same person who walked in. That's what the storm's all about." – Haruki Murakami**

**"When you pass through the waters, I will be with you…" – Isaiah 43:2 NIV**

~~~~~~~~~~~~~~~~~~~~~~~~~~

With Hurricane Irma forecasted to smash into Miami, Florida as a deadly category 5 hurricane, at my invitation, my college roommate and sister-friend Yaa, along with her husband Carl and their family quickly packed their essentials and fled their home in Miami to stay at our house in Central Florida. When they arrived, Carl jokingly remarked that they were not refugees, but Irma-gees.
~~~~~~~~~~~~~~~~~~~~~~~~~~

As the hurricane forecasts continued to roll in, I saw that Tampa, Florida was also projected to get a direct hit from Hurricane Irma. So, I invited my brother Kobina and his wife Barbara to leave their home in Tampa and join us as well. Soon we were ten Irma-gees at my house.

The news reports were frightening; Hurricane Irma was described as a *monster storm*, the likes of which hadn't been seen in the past century.

The Irma-gees from Miami had left no stone unturned in their preparations. They arrived at our house fully laden with food and emergency supplies and, fully knowledgeable about hurricanes. When they asked me a couple of questions about our hurricane prep, I felt challenged and immediately became defensive. I protested that those of us who lived in Central Florida didn't need to take the same level of hurricane precautions required for South Florida. "But we are expecting a massive South Florida-like hurricane in 24 hours!!" was their come back.

At this point I began to entertain serious fears that not only was I unprepared for this storm, but, now, I had potentially put the lives of two other families at risk by inviting them to seek shelter with us.

As my tension continued to mount, I began to observe everybody's 'behavior dysfunctions' (except my own, of course!). The 'interrogation' about our hurricane preparedness. My husband Eddie's curt response, "No, I'm not doing anything else to my house." Kobby's philosophical "People let's not lose sight of the fact that we are gathered here for a reason. What is the significance of this moment?" My sister-in-law Barbara (still a newlywed) made few comments and rather focused on watching the US Open Tennis championship. I imagined her wondering "What the heck kind of family have I married into?"

By Saturday afternoon, I recognized that we needed to change our focus from the size of the storm, to the size of our God. So, we gathered for family prayer time where I printed out a list of twelve short Bible verses talking about God's love and protection. A couple of those verses were taken from Psalm 91. All of us read the verses out loud, and then we each picked one verse that resonated with us and talked about it in the group.

We worshipped mainly to one song, *Yahweh*, written by Kofi Karikari. The lyrics of *Yahweh* are simple but incredibly powerful:

"We bow down and worship Yahweh.
Yahweh, Yahweh, Yahweh."

We discussed how 'Yahweh' is one of the names of God, and simply means "I am that I am". He is the God who had no beginning and has no end. The all-knowing, all-powerful, all-sufficient God.

We put our lives in Yahweh's hands and asked him to protect us, and all our homes (Davenport, Miami and Tampa) from the hurricane. We asked him to dispatch his angels to guard every single entrance and every single window of each of our homes and to protect us from the wind and rain. (He will order His angels to protect and guard you. – Luke 4:10 NLT).

We discussed that however God was going to do it, we would put our trust in Him, knowing that He would see us through this.

Having refocused, I personally began to feel a sense of peace and calm.

By late afternoon on Saturday September 9, we had experienced a couple of tornadoes with accompanying heavy rain. As dusk gave way to night, I looked out at our swimming pool and saw that it was brimming over into our lanai. I began to worry that the swimming pool's outlet may have been blocked or wasn't letting the water out fast enough. I could see the waters creeping ominously towards the house.

At that point I began to pray a simple prayer, *Lord, hold back the waters, so that they don't flood the house. If the outlet is somehow blocked, please unblock it!* I turned on the light in the lanai so that I could monitor the situation. I also touched (or pointed to) every window and door in my house and asked God to dispatch his angels to be on guard to secure them against the wind and rain.

As God is my witness, I looked at the lanai again five minutes later and saw, with my own eyes, that the waters had begun to recede, even as the rain continued to fall heavily.

Similarly, there were two spots in my house that I didn't realize had a leak: the window in my daughter Elissa's room, and a spot in our living room that sprayed a light mist during the heavy rains in the afternoon.

I prayed to God to protect those vulnerable areas. I placed towels in those areas.

After I prayed, I went to Elissa's room and saw that the towel on her window was completely soaked. So, I took that towel to the sink and wrung out the water. And then I replaced it with a new towel.

When I came downstairs, Yaa had finally gotten her kids to relax enough to be able to fall sleep. She told me that her youngest son, six-year-old Kevin, who had seemingly not paid attention during our prayer session, had asked his mother to look for "the Yahweh song" on YouTube. And then Kevin prayed, thanking God for saving us. (Note this is before the hurricane even hit.) After that, the boys were finally able to fall asleep.

Exhausted, I started to doze off on the sofa around 9pm...

I woke up at around 12.30 am. Most of us had gone to bed, but my brother Kobby had stayed awake and had continued to worship and pray. I joined him. We raised the volume of the music and simply sang the *Yahweh* song. Over and over and over again. Occasionally we would point to the windows and doors and the areas that had been leaking and ask God to protect us and all our homes from the wind and rain.

Oh, I forgot to mention that by this time, the forecasts had changed. The most dangerous part of the storm had bypassed Miami and Tampa and was now headed directly towards Polk County, where we live; forecast to hit us around 2 am.

At around 1 am, we gathered the children, still sleeping, to the safest part of the house. And we continued to pray. Mostly we just sang "the Yahweh song".

If there were loud and scary sounds, I didn't hear them. I was lost in my worship and I felt an incredible peace in my heart. It was one of the most beautiful moments of my life.

I guess it must have been around or just after 2 am that Carl, who was monitoring the hurricane, came to tell us that the storm had passed.

Our house was intact. No damage. No flooding. No loss of electricity or water. And all the towels I gathered the next morning were dry.

Kobby and Barbara's house in Tampa was intact. No damage. No flooding. No loss of electricity or water.

Carl and Yaa's house in Miami was intact. No damage. No flooding. No loss of electricity or water.

A couple of days later, I remembered that I had not picked up the towel from Elissa's window. I asked her where it was, and she responded that she had put the towel in her hamper. I started to tell her off for putting a water-soaked towel in her hamper, and her simple response to me was "No, Mom! The towel was dry!"

Don't tell me God is not real. I saw the receding waters. I felt the dry towels!

I learned a couple of lessons from this storm, that I will apply to other storms that may come my way:

1. It's good to be fully prepared for eventualities. However, know that there is a point at which additional information will not change your intended action, but will only serve to make you anxious. Why? Because your focus has been on the size of the storm (or the problem), rather than the size of your God. Know that point for yourself and switch your focus to the size of your God.

2. Based on the best forecasts, the Miami and Tampa Irma-gees left their homes and came to my house to escape a direct hit. Ironically, my house was actually the only one of the three homes that got hit directly. It reminds me of one of the Bible verses we read on Saturday:

The horse is prepared for the day of battle, but victory is with Yahweh (Proverbs 21:31 KJV).

God is indeed our Shield and Protector. I write this testimony in gratitude to Yahweh.

Sincerely, Aba.

# Miracle: The House Fire

**"Gye Nyame" ("Except for God") – an Adinkra symbol of the Akans of Ghana, which expresses the omnipotence and supremacy of God in all our affairs[8]**

**"…your whole self – spirit, soul, and body – will be kept safe…" – 1 Thessalonians 5:23 ERV**

~~~~~~~~~~~~~~~~~~~~~~~~~~

Do you believe in miracles? I do. I've experienced several. And I memorialize each one of them, because they give me faith to face the future.

Almost eighteen years ago, God spared my family from tragedy.

[8]Willis, W. Bruce. The Adinkra dictionary: a visual primer of the language of the Adinkra. Washington, D. C.: Pyramid Complex, 1998.
~~~~~~~~~~~~~~~~~~~~~~~~~~

It was a cold winter morning in Farmington, Connecticut. I was home with my babies, my mother and my sister, Ekua. My sister and I were on different extensions of my home phone, talking to a friend.

All of a sudden the smoke alarm came on, and the phone went dead. So, I ran through the house to investigate.

When I opened the door to the garage, I witnessed the most terrifying thick grey and black smoke, that filled the whole garage.

I immediately called 911 on the home phone, and we evacuated the building. In less than five minutes, fire trucks pulled up to my driveway.

Thankfully the fire damage was confined to only the garage. But I knew how blessed we had been; we lived in an older home that used oil for heating – and the oil tank was located in the garage!

I shudder to think of what could have happened if the oil tank had exploded.

But as if that wasn't a miracle in itself, read what happened next!

After a few hours we were allowed to return to the house. That's when I realized that the home phone wasn't working. So, I had the phone company come out the following day.

Within a few minutes of arrival, the Phone Guy came up to me and explained that extensive work had to be done to restore service, because the phone wire had been badly damaged; beyond repair.

I casually remarked, "I'm surprised, because I was able to call 911 on that phone."

And I will never forget what happened next. Phone Guy looked me straight in the eye and said "Ma'am, I am 100% sure that you could NOT have made any calls from this phone!"

Do you know what I believe? In my mind's eye I can even 'see' it – the Angel holding the phone wire together long enough for me to call 911!

This Bible verse comes to mind, whenever I think of my Christmas 2002 miracle:

"...And so no disaster will strike you, no violence will come near your home. God will put his angels in charge of you, to protect you wherever you go." (Psalm 91:10-11 GNT)

For anyone reading this, I pray that this same Protector-God keeps you and yours safe today and throughout this unprecedented time in our lives, that 2020 has come to represent. May He be your Safety in the face this Covid-19 pandemic, your Provider in this season of global economic downturn, and your Peace through all the changes that 2020 has brought to our lives.

May God open your eyes to see the amazing miracles He is working in your life each and every day!

## *Leave Room*

**(December 31, 2019)**

**"Call to Me, and I will answer you…" – Jeremiah 33:3 NIV**

**"There are only two ways to live your life. One, as though nothing is a miracle. The other as though everything is a miracle." – Albert Einstein**

~~~~~~~~~~~~~~~~~~~~~~~~~~~~~~

My first reaction to things is often hilarious. Over the years my family has had many good laughs, because of this.

About a year ago, a new gas station opened up near my house and I decided to check it out. As I walked into the store, I was immediately drawn to their sophisticated touch-screen coffee machines. Although I'm not a big coffee drinker, they
~~~~~~~~~~~~~~~~~~~~~~~~~~~~~~

looked so impressive to me that I decided to get a cup of coffee.

I began to make my selection:
*Drink: coffee.*
*Cup: small.*

The next screen gave me two options:
*"Fill Cup"* or *"Leave Room"*.

My brain didn't immediately process the second option, and so - true story - my first thoughts were "Leave room? And go where?? Why can't I stay in here? How long will this coffee take to brew, anyway?"

After a few seconds, though, it eventually dawned on me that while the "Fill Cup" option filled the cup to the brim with freshly brewed coffee, the "Leave Room" option left space in the cup to allow one to add milk, cream, or whatever flavorings one desired to add to their coffee.

As funny (and embarrassing to share) as that moment was, the experience took on a deeper meaning for me.

You can choose to fill your cup to the brim with unadulterated, aromatic, freshly brewed coffee.

Or, you could choose to leave room in your cup to add milk/cream/flavorings to give yourself a different – and, some might argue, a better – coffee drinking experience.

Life is often like a rollercoaster; filled with hills and valleys. 2019 was a very blessed year for me and mine. But the year also presented some challenges. And I'm still shaken by the loss of my dear brother-friend a few weeks ago.

The state of the world concerns me. Intolerance, hatred, racial injustice, political unrest, fighting, corruption and poverty are widespread. And it hurts my heart to hear about the burdens that so many people are carrying.

Life can be tough. I personally could not do life without God. Like David in Psalms 27:13 NKJV, "I would have lost heart unless I had believed that I would see the goodness of the Lord in the land of the living."

I have realized that I need to leave room in my life for the God who is my Shepherd, my Healer, my Provider, my Victory, my Friend, my Restorer, and my Peace. It is non-negotiable for me.

I encourage you to do so as well.

Leave room for God's grace and mercy. It makes a huge difference to our lives.

Leave room for God to be the source of your strength, your joy, your provision and your healing.

Leave room to know that His blessings will manifest in your life at His appointed time.

Leave room to trust that, in difficult seasons, as you take life one step at a time, His direction will surely come.

Leave room for His miracles to get you through impossible situations. His miracles are real, if only you believe.

Leave room to be grateful when He disciplines you, knowing that His correction is always for your good.

Leave room to understand that setbacks are actually opportunities to regroup, change course and move in the direction of the life for which you were purposed.

Above all, leave room for Hope in your life. Remember that He will take care of you, NO MATTER what you are going through.

"... I'll show up and take care of you as I promised... I know what I'm doing. I have it all planned out—plans to take care of you, not abandon you, plans to give you the future you hope for." (Jeremiah 29:11 MSG)

Leave Room!

Fill Cup
Leave Room

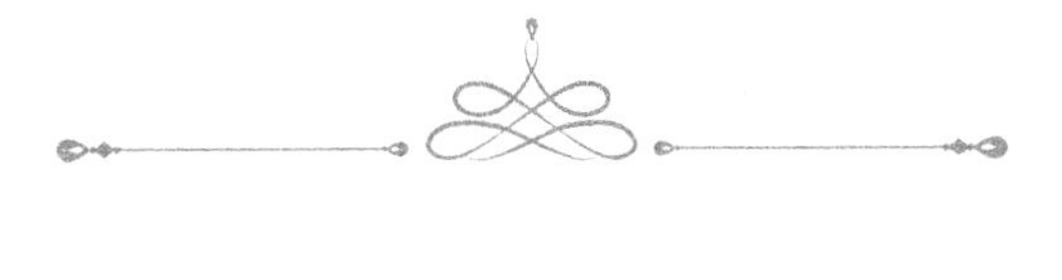

# Reviews

## REVIEW BY CHARLOTTE AMA OSEI

I felt honoured and privileged to be asked to write a review of this amazing book by Aba Andah. Of course, this was until I actually read the book and I realized, just how difficult it would be to properly capture the essence of the book.

Aba's book is at once a manual for life, as well as a call for a return to first principles: loving God, living a life of purpose and understanding the depth of God's love. Aba reminds us, in a gentle yet unmissable manner, that our faith cannot be separated from any aspect of our lives: work, marriage, ministry, family and relationships. And so her faith, in very practical ways, is demonstrated in the big issues as well as the little things of life and her faith is woven into the tapestry of her life as a wife, mother, professional, daughter, sister, friend and neighbor. She tackles the big issues with such candour and amazing humane-ness: abortion, infidelity, absentee dads, values, legacy issues and living life intentionally.

I was encouraged and inspired to live better and leave a stronger legacy by *Reflections of A Hopemonger* and I am incredibly proud to call Aba my sister and my friend.

*Mrs. Charlotte Ama Osei*
*Lawyer & International Elections Consultant*
*Former Electoral Commissioner of Ghana*

## REVIEW BY ACE ANAN ANKOMAH

It must have been somewhere in January 1994 when I first met Aba. Although it appears that we had both been on the campus of the University of Ghana, Legon for about a year, we did not meet or know each other then. But I had been at Queen's University in Kingston, Ontario, Canada for one semester, and the second semester was just beginning. Kingston, Ontario was cold, especially for an African student. International students generally hung out at the John Deutsch International Students Centre. My main attraction there was to meet other International students (as in people who looked like me) and to play on the upright piano there. One day a young lady entered the Centre, and it took just one look to guess that she might be Ghanaian too. When she spoke, all doubts dissipated. But the most striking feature: the colours of her earmuffs – bright mauve and a brighter red. I surmised she was either Asante or Ewe, on account of those colours. Partially wrong. She was Fante AND Ewe (with some Akwapim thrown into the mix).

That began a friendship that has spanned all of these years. Aba is irritatingly passionate, deep and reflective. This is probably born out of her many sides. Just look at her educational qualifications: Bachelors in Biochemistry; then MBA; then MA and a few other consonants behind her name ("can I buy a vowel?") I call her a magician!

Her passion shows in this book *Reflections of A Hopemonger.* In this title she sets hope up as a commodity and she as the dealer in it. Her theme is therefore made apparent in the title, and she promotes hope throughout the book. Obama has his *Audacity of Hope.* But welcome unto the stage the most incurable optimist that I have met in my life, who casts herself as a dealer in the commodity called 'Hope'.

She starts by waxing definitional, setting us up with what she considers a "good story," that is "one that carries a lesson, which leads us to new insights and a better way of living." Thus, you might have a story; but it is just a story. It does not cross the threshold that deserves the qualifier "good" (forget better, best or excellent) unless it is "authentic" and reveals "our character defects and unfolds with blood, sweat, tears, missteps, failures, persistence, resilience and, then, victory." It is like a flowchart. Thus, she sets you up for a no-holds-barred and no-punches-pulled set of stories, narratives and anecdotes that leave you reflective and dazed sometimes. I promise you your "phew, did she say THAT?" moments.

She tells us that even the imperfect has a value. She says, "the truth, though, is that it is our imperfect, gritty authentic personal stories that people identify with and actually learn from." In *Diamond Incentive,* she wins a flawless diamond at work, showing how hard work can eliminate self-doubt. In *Collateral Damage,* she dreams of a red corvette. Well, remember one of the colours of her earmuffs? But the story is not about cars at all. It is about giving up on something you very badly want to do, because of the harm it could or would bring to loved ones. *Wounds of a Friend* teaches that you need friends not just to make you happy, but also to tell you the truth, even where it hurts. Tough, but a life lesson.

She skillfully shows how her life is completely woven around her family and friends, by weaving them into the story and holding very little or nothing back. The Reflections are so comprehensive that even I get a mention in *Some Have Entertained Angels,* even though I won't mention my name and "angel" within 30 paragraphs of each other. Yes, I remember those 'cheap Tuesday' movies. Sometimes, together with other broke students, we watched two movies on the same night. If Aba considers me an angel, then she is really, truly and hopelessly a *Hopemonger*. Obama, take a back seat. The real deal is here. But the lesson is clear. You may never be able to tell the end of a thing from its beginning. Be kind to all you meet.

Although I am sorely tempted to review every chapter of the book, I am not going to do that. You need to buy it; you need to read it. What I say in conclusion is that by the time you are done, this hopemonger, the incurable dealer in hope would have you nailing your flag to her mast of hope and her central theme that even "character defects… blood, sweat, tears, missteps, failures, persistence, resilience" are just precursors to the ultimate, VICTORY!

*Ace Anan Ankomah*
*Managing Partner*
*Head of Litigation, Arbitration & Dispute Resolution Practice*
*Bentsi-Enchill, Letsa & Ankomah*
*Ghana*

## REVIEW BY KWAME KURANKYI DADSON

Aba's book is a masterpiece of honesty, therapy and from-the-heart advice.

Weaving a tapestry of autobiographical stories, she speaks openly about how her experiences have shaped her life. From tales of pushy acquaintances to enigmatic neighbors, we find ourselves immersed into her minutest struggles, sharing victories, joys and fears.

For a book with a decent amount of biblical reference, it does not at all come across as preachy. Aba's family are close friends with whom I have met up with on far fewer occasions in the last two decades than I would have liked, due to the physical distances between us. However, whenever we have had the pleasure, she has shown a maturity that comes across clearly in the book. It is an unusual talent, to keep the reader's attention with life-coaching advice while remaining open, yet vulnerable and not detached. Her close connection to her immediate and wider family and network of core friends is laid open to us and each little story is a lesson that illuminates with a simple but relevant message.

*Reflections of A Hopemonger* is paradoxical. On first browsing it seems a mere 'light read' and is certainly easy to go through, but is so much deeper than that, and one that lends itself to multiple pulls from the shelf to get the most out of it.

Aba writes just as she lives – generously and with thoughtful care. It would be churlish of me to try to single out stories, as each is excellent in its own way, but a few that resonated with me are the humorous but insightful encounter with Dalal in *If Pleasing People Were My Goal*, the wise restraining counsel of *Lord, Slap All My Enemies In The Face* and the haunting reality of *And Who is My Neighbor?*

I highly recommend it for people of all faiths and worldviews as the truths it reveals affect us all. You will devour it and put it down, I guarantee, more hopeful than before.

*Kwame Kurankyi Dadson*
*Family friend and fellow writer*
*Chief Operations Officer, CoreNett Ltd*

**REVIEW BY ESI E. ANSAH**

In this very engaging collection of reflections, Aba shares candid reflections that take you down a path where you stop to pick beautiful expressions as you would flowers; walk a little faster, anxious to read and know more, linger awhile along the way, race ahead in some parts, all the while savoring the journey.

The collection is laced with scripture, and is instructive, but certainly not preachy. It's captured in such a way that one can nibble a piece at a time, savor the flavor, and then return for more. That makes the book an easy read that can travel with the reader anywhere.

First, the reflections are very relatable, and she allows us to experience everyday life through her eyes. The essay on *Voices* is a great reminder of the inner battles we all fight, and the need to recognize and manage them effectively. We can see many of our own experiences in her accounts, such as the story of Dalal the "few groceries" friend whom we all have, and the practical lessons to be picked for our own journeys in managing relationships.

In this collection, one will see and experience variety – from references to Rudyard Kipling to Bob Marley to Jesus Christ, Beyonce and others. Aba creates enough room for us to learn from them all in this mosaic of great lessons.

It is refreshing and inspiring to see her humanity in some of the reflections, and her courage in sharing some of her own toughest life experiences especially with family life. She gracefully introduces us to her parents, sharing her growing-up struggles with her mom, the simplicity of her dad's life, the blessing of her sibling support-system, the pains and pleasures of marriage, celebrating her husband (look out for, and enjoy the piece on the Light Soup!), and playing Alpha Mom to wonderful children.

Overall, this is an enjoyable book worth reading; it will bring outbursts of laughter, moments of jaws dropping, silent smiles, perhaps a few watery eyes and most importantly, inspiration and great lessons.

*Dr. Esi E. Ansah*
*Lecturer, Ashesi University*
*CEO, Axis Human Capital Ltd*

**REVIEW BY ESI EDUAFOWA SEY**

From the very first page, *Reflections of A Hopemonger* invites you to plunge in, at the deep end. Aba wastes no time paddling at the shallow edges of the whirlpool of her life or yours. But with a firm hand, a brave heart and a twinkle in her eye, she takes your hand in hers, and asks, "Do you dare jump in, with me?"

And jump you will, for who can resist the allure of a storyteller, or the craft of a hopemonger who re-writes her life story, and yours, even as she tells it; revitalizing each failed experience with the lessons you missed, each moment of laughter with the joy that so quickly faded, and re-playing for you, the song of life in its starkness, its painfulness, yet its ever-beautiful hopefulness.

So, her prologue already tells it as it is, alerting you of what is to come in the chapters ahead. Before you can say, *hey where's my selfie-stick?* Aba captures your attention with a blunt reminder of the shallowness of the perfect lives we present on the outside, and the richness of the depths we keep on the inside. The richness of the experience of pain, of ill health, of failure, of embarrassment and of loss; depths rich with lessons we could learn and live and share, but which we miss out on, as we pose for the perfectly made-up moments on the social media pages of our lives.

Not so in Aba's reflections on life and living it. She touches on taboo topics – the dreaded suspicion, the awful truth, the ultimate loss from infidelity exposed, and then the healing and restoration. She wades into our uglier emotions – the shadow of spitefulness that seeps through the cracks of a broken home and spreads ripples of far-reaching damage on the ex-husband and the beloved daughter he has been barred from seeing.

Aba speaks of the unspeakable – the abortion we turned a conveniently blind eye to, or that niggling feeling that this friend of ours only shows up when they need something from us; that we might be on a one-way street friendship, which, like the WhatsApp groups that drain our energies, we dare not exit.

But that is not where it ends. To every chapter of *Reflections of A Hopemonger*, there is a principle, which we may carry away with us as we turn the page on the chapter; a nugget of wisdom to guide our words, our actions and even our emotions, as we look up from its pages and speak to that colleague, or son, or mother-in-law, or spouse.

Those principles are like the pollen that lies on the stamen of a flower, and Aba, a joyfully industrious hummingbird, fluttering from flower to flower, picking, spreading and scattering grains of pollinated wisdom where they may germinate and produce and re-produce.

There are principles you already know, but forget when you need them most, like "you'll never be able to please all the people all the time".

And others you actually never thought of, like the beauty of the semi-colon.

So, whom is this book meant for?

It is for the eldest son, feeling the weight of his parents' high expectations of him. Read *Custodian.*

It is for the stay-at-home mum, with an amazingly simple idea for a business she could manage from home, but who is too scared to try it out, because maybe, it won't work out. Read *One Talent Servant.*

It is for the middle-aged man, scared of the look he sees in his daughter's eyes, as he lashes out the pain of unfulfilled dreams and plans upon his wife's shoulders and back, and yet helpless, it seems, to break the pattern of aggression and violence that he is weaving into his own home. And his wife, lashing back with a tongue as fiery and destructive as red molten from an erupting volcano. Read *Collateral Damage.*

It is for the professional, caught in a spiral of work, work, work, work, work, and work. Read *To Don't List.*

And it is for the young husband, contemplating adding snails and perhaps a few crabs to the chicken soup he purposely came home early to prepare as a surprise for his wife on her return from her first day at work after maternity leave. Read *Chicken Light Soup for an Effutu Soul.*

How should you read *Reflections of A Hopemonger*? Let me count the ways…

You can read it as an accompaniment to your daily devotional or during those precious quiet minutes of your day when you finally get to sit by yourself for a half hour, just to think or not think.

You can splurge on this book; read it from cover to cover, underlining the phrases and sentences and paragraphs that grab you, as you read along. Cautionary word: you are likely to find you underlined the whole book right through.

You can recommend it to your book club and read it alongside your favorite friends and then discuss. Be prepared though, for yourself, your friendships, and your book club, to never be quite the same again.

What is left to say now, by way of review, except that I can guarantee you will begin this book, reading about Aba and her life and times, but you will end it having read about yourself. And then, as you reach the final chapter and turn the final page, you will find yourself picking up the next chapter of your life, with a certain something that wasn't there when you began reading – a distinct, unmistakable and uncompromisingly bright glimmer of hope.

*Esi Eduafowa Sey, PhD*
*Organization Development Practitioner*
*& Childhood Friend*

## REVIEW BY EKUA CATO THOMSON

Thank you for writing *Reflections of a Hopemonger*, Aba! Thank you for the pearls of wisdom, the life lessons, the spiritual values, the humor, and the awesome thought-provoking moments within these pages! What should we make of our life experiences, if not to learn from them?

In *Reflections of a Hopemonger*, Aba delves deeply, not only into her own experiences, but also into what the experiences of others have taught her. Aba is vulnerable and transparent in sharing these truths, so that the reader, in turn, can learn from them.

In *Reflections of a Hopemonger*, Aba shares not only the "what", but also suggestions on the "how to".

There truly is something for everyone in this book. Who doesn't need to write a "To Don't List"?

*Reflections of a Hopemonger* reveals real, authentic, insightful thoughts and musings about self, relationships, friendships, marriage, and even a cup of coffee!

Faith abounds! Hope abounds! This book is a must read! You will find yourself revisiting specific chapters and using the wisdom gleaned to help you in wide range of life situations.

The purpose of *Reflections of a Hopemonger* is clear: the reader cannot help but be challenged, moving forward, to live with mindful intention and purpose!

*Ekua Cato Thomson*
*Clinical Social Worker*

## REVIEW BY DAPHNE MARTINSON-LARBI

A collection of essays lovingly placed into a beautifully wrapped, dainty, tissue-filled gift box. A unique time capsule.

That for me, is Aba's *Reflections of a Hopemonger*.

Every page offered a little priceless nugget for me to place in my treasure box of thoughts, notes-to-self, affirmation and hope boosters and I found myself reaching for my phone to capture those words that would simply not let me go.

Aba bravely invites you into her life to walk enormous portions of her journey beside her. A thought-provoking and delicately woven piece of work.

*Daphne Martinson-Larbi*
*Wellness Coach & Oncology Massage Therapist*

## REVIEW BY KOBINA SAMORE CATO

*Reflections of A Hopemonger* is for the reader who is open to reflection and growth. It provides the fertile ground where mind and spirit collide in their quest to extract meaning out of experience, ultimately birthing faith and hope.

Aba places the spotlight on herself in this book, as she explores facets of her life, her past interactions, her beliefs and her behaviours. With honesty and transparency she wades into deep waters and enters into some not so flowery places.

Aba masterfully tackles the tough issues of her life. She teaches the reader that one does not have to be defined by one's difficult experiences. And often, through difficult experiences, it is possible to discover one's purpose.

She shares thought-provoking personal stories; compelling enough to convince even the most diehard cynic that one's capacity for hope can always be expanded.

Who should read *Reflections Of A Hopemonger*? By the end of the book, these three questions kept echoing in my mind:

Do you want to have the courage to look yourself in the mirror and say, "I am more than the sum of my difficult experiences"?

Do you want to experience deeper life connections?

Do you want to live a life of greater significance?

If you answered *yes* to any of these, then without hesitation, *Reflections Of A Hopemonger* is the book for you.

*Kobina Samore Cato*
*Education Management Professional & Certified Professional Coach*

## REVIEW BY ADELINE AIDOO AINOOSON

***Reflections of A Hopemonger*** welcomes the reader to have a seat in the currently most sought after spot on earth - a place of hope. In these days of the coronavirus pandemic, hope is an essential commodity to be purchased at any price. To excite/fuel this sale, Aba takes on the challenge of baring her personal life. This takes courage in the knowledge of her purpose, and a continuous flow of the oil of God's grace on her life. Aba's sole purpose is to bring insight for positive change. ***Reflections of A Hopemonger*** is an eye opener and like the writer, is candid in character.

As you journey through the pages of ***Reflections of A Hopemonger***, you will begin to look differently at the ***semicolon***; beyond its use as a punctuation mark, to also as a strong and charming link, connecting you to the days ahead with hope. You will be encouraged with such demonstrative language to ***leave room*** for God in a way that enables the reader to visualize God coming in and taking His place. God will then perform His miraculous acts in your life and you will ***remember*** to build a memorial in His honor.

Aba cautions the reader on the different ways in which one 'escapes' from a marriage and continuously draws the reader into appreciating what I reflect on as the golden lesson, that is - no matter how right you are, you have absolutely NO RIGHT to do ***a-b-c-d-e and/or f***.

She captures the ***'spoilers'*** of the bible in an interesting narration, to heighten our hope, as we already know how those situations ended. She talks about those seemingly unending ***tunnels*** along this journey of life and infuses enough hope to assure the reader that they can't last forever.

My best take from ***Reflections of a Hopemonger is this*** - if there is ever one thing of which having too much can never be bad, it is hope. Hope is the lifeline to God.

***Reflections of a Hopemonger*** is written with a perfect blend of the unspoken professional notion of a psychotherapist and a firm believer in the faithfulness of an omnipotent, omnipresent and omniscient God. Next to whatever book one holds dear should be a copy of ***Reflections of A Hopemonger***.

Now sit back, relax, pour yourself a glass of wine (or juice or water) and enjoy the taste of a hope-filled world, served by ***Reflections of A Hopemonger***.

Thank you Aba and on life's unsteady trail may your hope and trust in the Lord's faithfulness always bring you to the expected end.

Much praise for this book Aba! Kudos!

*Adeline Aidoo Ainooson*
*Attorney-at-Law*
*Former Investigator, U.S. Department of Homeland Security*

Connect with The Author Online:

Facebook: @abacatoandah1
Instagram: @abacatoandah
Twitter: @abacatoandah
LinkedIn: @abacatoandah
Email: hopemonger.aba@gmail.com

Made in USA - Kendallville, IN
1187465_9789988902308
10.29.2020 1310